INSPIRING STORIES

FOR YOUNG ATHLETES

A Collection of Unbelievable Stories about Mental Toughness,

Confidence and How to Overcome Fears & Gain the Mindset of Winners

CATHY SUSMAN

Author: Cathy Susman
illustrator: Oriol San Julian - Team of dibustock.com

Table of Contents

INTRODUCTION

Being a boy and/or a male athlete in today's society isn't a walk in the park. We all know that it's complex, challenging, and stressful at times. Yet as we transition from boys to men, we can ensure that we move mindfully, morally, intentionally, happily, healthily, and ethically. From important topics and life lessons about persistence, focus, self-belief, bravery, concentration, healing, determination, grit, resilience, a growth and champion mindset, confidence, and other necessary social skills, you'll uncover a treasure chest of gems in this book.

You'll soon discover some valuable tips to speak, act, and think like a leader. You'll learn how and why practice is a superpower in sports and life, how to be optimistic, collaborative, empathetic, and other empowering attributes. You'll gain stealth mental health ability and socioemotional depth.

Dive in and discover not only sensational sports stories about swimming, chess, boxing, figure skating, soccer, cycling, surfing, hockey, but also all friendship and family themes.

The practical post-reading activities will also allow you to interact closely with these concepts in creative, multidisciplinary, and engaging ways.

You'll also greatly hone your geography skills as we travel to diverse places like sunny Florida, gorgeous Boulder, Colorado, urban Detroit, happy Hawaii, arid New Mexico, lively Philadelphia, PA, breath-taking Utah, USA.

Are you ready now to get set, go, and glow today, the mindful way?

CHAPTER 1

"Surf on Your Turf: Zain Gains Persistence and Focus"

Are you ready to catch some wild waves in stunning Hawaii today? You can also practice your hula dancing, try some local pineapple or coconut juice (yummy!), and wear a colorful lei to celebrate local Polynesian culture. Then you'll uncover surfing and much, much more in this educational and entertaining tale, "Surf on Your Turf: Zain Gains Persistence and Focus."

First off, join Zain, an outgoing, confident, friendly, bold, brave, and skilled surfing star as he explores life lessons and finds lots of fun in the sun during his character education experience. His young success story is absolutely inspirational. It's closely related to the vital character trait of maintaining focus to concentrate fully on our dreams, objectives, and goals in life. Doesn't that sound as exciting as a luau or a tour to a local volcano?

With a clear sense of focus, you can be like Zain as you fully pay attention to your targeted objectives and never waver. When you act, speak, think, and lead with focus, you also mindfully and totally use and immerse in all of your five senses to attain what you want. Can you name the five sense here now? Will you spot them in the story when Zain exhibits them?

So let's be brave and catch a wave of wonder in this action packed, immersive, and enjoyable story. Watch clever, creative, and patient Zain as he acquires a better understanding of what persistence is and why it can help you to proactively pursue your goals.

No, it's not a new type of sushi. Persistence is sort of like a life raft to me; it means that you hang on tightly and continue to do something, even when it seems too hard or too impossible. Like persevere, persistence is a bit similar to a GPS on one's phone or in a car: it allows you to stay on track and navigate toward your dreams and goals because persistence lets you last and exist in what you really want to achieve. Are you ready to survive and thrive with Zain?

Whether you want to surf, scuba dive, snorkel, or swim, please note that your aspirations should always be your top priority. You should never give up or forget to work on your dreams and goals because of any slight changes, obstacles, or difficulties that you may encounter in the process. Beware of sharks in those waters, right?

In other words, just ride the waves of life with confidence and tenacity as this story so cleverly models. Follows Zain's brave surfing mindset as he attempts to find and ride the biggest wave in the world!

A cool way to remember persistence is this mindful mantra: If you persist with confidence and focus, you'll resist quitting or failure. Persist not to resist! It's like giving yourself a permission slip or a pass to success! Can you try reciting it 10 times? What other creative ways will you use and apply to remember these valuable life lessons? Mahalo!

Aloha! It was a sweltering summer day on a glorious little island in Hawaii. An athletic boy named Zain, and his father, Jozi, made their way to the shore.

Zain loved to walk on the prickly sand with his surfboard, enter the water, hop on the board, and surf with the competitive spirit of a shark, propelling him forward.

In fact, ever since he was a baby, he adored the ocean. Before he took his first few steps, he had already learned to swim in the sea. The locals nicknamed him "Water baby!"

As Zain grew older, he would go to the beach to watch the azure blue waters. The sunshine made the water in the ocean sparkle, and the mere sight of this made his little heart happy. Jozi taught Zain every sea sport, but it was clear that Zain would be a great surfer.

During childhood every evening after school, Zain would happily go to the shore and surf. The water on his skin and the wind blowing his hair made him feel so focused, free, and confident.

All at once, he had an brilliant epiphany—he wanted to find and ride the largest wave in Hawaii. So, that evening, as the sun was setting, he dashed home and told his father, "Papa, I want to ride the biggest wave in the world!"

Jozi stood in disbelief. He couldn't believe that his little boy was more courageous, persistent, and focused than most.

"Son, your dream is as big as the Pacific Ocean, but that doesn't mean it's not possible," Jozi replied. His father always encouraged Zain and made him believe that nothing was impossible in life.

He also tried to give Zain everything he needed because his mother worked in Honolulu, far from the tiny island where they. Papa tried to be the only source of support that Zain needed, but it was clear that the young boy needed his mother, too.

Eventually, Papa had to make a tough decision. He decided it was time to move to the city, so Zain could have a full family by his side. It was the healthiest thing to do, even though it would break Zain's heart since he adored the beach.

Instead of tall palm trees, the city had tall skyscrapers. In place of an ocean that stretched toward other countries, the city had too many tourists. Swapping organic, healthy fresh fruits and vegetables, the city had way more frozen foods-yuck! Truthfully, Zain would eventually adapt to city life, but at what cost? His surfing dreams?

Thoughts raced through Zain's confused mind, but he was an understanding child. Therefore, he let it go and accepted his fate with his signature surfer focus and Polynesian persistence!

"Zain? Did you pack all your belongings?" Papa asked.

"Yes, Dad! I'm ready!" Zain replied as he hurriedly walked downstairs.

The duo hailed a cab to the airport. Upon arrival, Zain was in awe at the sight of massive airplanes. He was merely used to seeing large ships that floated on the water, but the plane could literally float in the air!

As a result, Zain was super impressed since his heart was extremely adventurous. Even though he would be unable to see the ocean, at least his new path in life would be filled with exciting and new experiences.

He remains close to Pap as they enter the waiting area and are shortly called upon to board their flight. Then they walk toward the plane and find their seat. Immediately after, the plane takes off.

Zain sat by the window. The view below was beautiful; the ocean looked so gigantic. After a few hours, he and his Dad arrived in the busiest city, Honolulu. The city center was jam-packed with people. It was a hub of activity, and everyone was trying to do something. Zain's mother, Dora, came to pick them up and cheerfully drove them to their new house.

As the days passed, Zain tried to suppress the fact that he missed living on the island but grew sadder with each passing day. His biggest dream was to surf Hawaii's largest wave, and he started crafting a plan that would work. With focus and persistence, he knew that he would excel!

One day, he puzzled his mother by asking a direct question. "Mother, can you take me to a surfing beach?"

"Don't you miss the ocean?" He added.

His mother smiled and replied, "Why do you want to go to the beach? Yes, I miss the ocean all the time!"

"Then can we go back to the Island?" Zain begged.

"You're still young, so you don't understand that there are responsibilities!" Dora emphasized.

"But.." Before he could finish the sentence, his mother left the room and returned with an album filled with pictures of him surfing a massive wave.

"Mama! Where's this?" Zain's eyes glowed with excitement.

"It's somewhere that's important to me; it was on the island many years ago!" Dora explained.

Their conversation made Zain feel more at ease. He bonded with his mother in the best way possible, giving Zain the newfound strength to persist a few more days until city life slowly made him miserable.

In response, he voiced his serious concerns to his parents, who agreed they'd let him join surfing competitions and visit the remote beaches during weekends to practice.

Zain eagerly waited for the weekend to arrive, and finally, it was the eve before the special day. Excitement sprinted through his body, making him stay awake throughout the night.

The following day, the sun's ray's flickered through Zain's bedroom window, waking him up to get ready for the day. He packed his surfboard and swim trunks and went with his dad to the bus station, where they would then catch a bus to the remote beaches since it was more affordable.

As they arrived, the salty air made Zain feel alive. The atmosphere in the city was too congested, and he savored the breeze.

Then the duo went to the beach and practiced all day. At night, they slept at Uncle Pako's house and practiced more surfing the next day.

Even though hard work was necessary to achieve his dreams, Zain didn't care. He continued with focus and persistence.

Once the day ended, they took a bus that night and went back to the city. This continued for weeks, months, and then years. His parents signed Zain up when he was old enough to join a surfing competition. It would be held on the island, and both of parents would accompany Zain. It was even more exciting this time since his parents saved some money and they'd be flying to the remote beaches this time.

Upon landing, they all went to the beach together and enjoyed their day. The following day was the Regional Championship game, so Zain woke up early and went surfing.

In reality, his biggest dream was not to win gold medals; instead, it was to surf the largest wave in the world. Because this was his starting point, he had to win.

The audience eagerly gathered at the beach. It was also the turtle egg hatching season and everyone enjoyed the special sight.

Soon after, the contestants lined up and plunged into the water. The whistle was blown and the surfers began to swim in order to catch a gigantic wave.

Guess who went to catch a huge wave? Zain's heart beat fast since this was his first competition. The wind hit his face with mighty blows, but he didn't fall beneath the waves. Instead, he was steady, focused, and persistent while riding the wicked wave, making the crowd cheer. Eventually, he won the competition and proudly earned his first gold medal.

Zain's excitement then took the best of him. He was thrilled to be victorious and the sky was the limit. His parents were proud and returned to the Honolulu super happy.

As years went by, he matured into a strong young man led by faith. He believed his ultimate dream would soon come true.

Throughout the years, he had managed to gather several medals. Plus, with the money earned from the competitions, he decided to pursue his dream as soon as he turned 18. His parents supported this dream because Zain's heart was in the right place as well as focused and persistent.

Next, he celebrated his 18th birthday as his parents transported him to the world's largest surfing competition preparation area. He soon learned that the weather forecast predicted the biggest wave in the world within the next five days.

The journey was long and tedious, but it would be totally worth it in the end. Zain started socializing with local surfers, hoping he would be directed to the only man who had survived the largest wave in the world. Zain was hoping he would be the next one.

"So, who are you and what are you looking for?" A local surfer asked.

"I'm Zain, but I'm looking for Zahi." Zain confidently replied.

The man started laughing hysterically. "And what makes you think Zahi wants to see you?"

Zain quickly announced, "Because I'll ride the biggest wave in the world in 5 days!"

The man's laugh disappeared; instead, he stared at the young man in front of him and told him to follow along. "To meet Zahi, you'll have to wait." The man explained.

"How long?" Zain asked.

"However long it takes," The man replied.

"But, I'm supposed to surf in five days!" Zain argued.

They arrived at a small hut. The man offered cold water to drink. "Thanks." Zain said.

"He's the only one who'll tell you all you need to know. Before surfing, you must meet him!" The man insisted.

After they both waited for hours that night, Zahi did not show up. So the following day, Zain decided to return to the hotel to freshen up. But as he was leaving, he met an odd-looking man with an eye patch. Could he be a pirate?

"Another surfer who wants to ride the wave?" He mumbled as he hobbled away.

Zain persistently followed the man.

"Every dreamer I've met didn't survive, except me," he continued.

"Zahi?" Zain asked.

"Yes, it's me. So, what do you want to know?" Zahi asked.

"Everything!" Zain replied.

The old man chuckled and praised, "Wow, I like your spirit!"

Zahi sat with Zain in the hut and described everything he needed to know. "Knowledge is important, but it won't save you. You must be ambitious, focused, and persistent enough to ride the wave like there's no tomorrow," Zahi advised.

Zain sincerely thanked Zahi and returned to the hotel room, where he called his parents to let them know he was doing fine.

During the next few days, he went to the ocean every day to practice.

On the last day, however, something unusual happened. Zahi was at the beach, watching him surf the waves.

"Why did you come?" Zain asked.

"You remind me of myself. I feel drawn to you. Something tells me you're special," Zahi answered.

"As you surf the waters tomorrow, you must merge and become one with it. Only then will it not swallow you. The board is just a piece equipment: what matters is how lightweight, focused, calm, and persistent you are when on it. Don't be tense!" Zahi added.

"Thank you for your incredible advice!" Zain thanked him once again.

Finally, the day arrived, and Zain went to the beach with his board to wait for the biggest wave. Just as he was about to give up and head home, he could not believe it—there it was! A gigantic wave!

Without hesitation, he jumped into the water and could feel the weight of water slapping against his body, which only made him more focused and motivated to chase after the wild wave.

The passersby stopped to watch in disbelief; some even whipped out their phones to record. As Zain got closer to the wave, he started feeling anxious; the tide was too big! Would he be able to ride it? Surfers never think about their last wave but at this time, he wondered if he would truly survive this massive feat.

Just when he was about to let doubts plant seeds in his mind, he remembered what Zahi had said. Zain had to merge with the water and become one with persistence and focus, so he stood on his surfboard and rode against the wave, letting go of all the tension in his body.

It was exactly as he had imagined! The wave was perfect! The freedom he felt as a child was unleashed; in this instance, he felt it more than ever before! At this moment, life was worth living!

He joyfully rode the wave until it disappeared. It felt as though he was in his own dream world. Yet as soon as he came back to reality, he heard cheers from the crowd. Zain thought getting recognition as the surfer who rode the biggest wave would make him happy, but that wasn't the case. His true satisfaction was knowing that persistence, patience, and focus led him to this impressive feat.

Learned lessons

As you just read, nothing is ever truly impossible in life when you apply these vital life lessons and character traits. In reality, all you have to do is believe in yourself to achieve your goals, objectives, dreams, desires. Please hold fast to this truth that nothing is ever too big for you!

Just like no wave is too big for Zain, always make a splash in life with determination and passion, You, too, can achieve success when your heart is in the right place. Always remember to be persistent and focused at whatever you set your mind and heart to obtain!

Based on this story's valuable lessons, please never feel like you aren't strong, good, or worthy enough just because you might not look like the other typical athletes in your chosen sport. You shouldn't allow yourself to be trapped by other people's shallow opinions or rigid expectations of you. Always aim to please yourself first, not others.

Here are some final reflections and free bonus gift activities to apply the outstanding character education and life lessons from the story, "Surf on Your Turf: Zain Gains Persistence and Focus:"

1. **Surf's Up:** Scan the story again and locate 2-3 new vocabulary words related to surfing. Try to say and spell them aloud. Practice using them in an original sentence.

   _____

   _____

2. **Hocus Pocus Focus:** What does the vital character trait of maintaining focus mean to you? How does it help Zain in life and in surfing? Can you recall a time in your life when you used focus to find freedom and success?

   _____

   _____

3. **Focus Flower:** When we act, speak, think, and lead with focus in our lives, we can mindfully and totally use and

immerse in all of our five senses. Draw a flower and label each petal with a goal that you seek to attain. Refer to this flower when you need to practice your focus daily

---

_____

_____

4. Name Game: Review the story again. What did the locals nickname Zain? Do you have a nickname? If so, what does it mean? Who gave it to you?

_____

_____

5. Dream Team: Name the characters who helped Zain to achieve his dreams. Who were they? Who is on your dream team of support and love in life?

_____

_____

CHAPTER 2

"Get Your Head In The Game: Kai's Hockey Happiness and Lesson in Determination and Acceptance"

Have you ever heard the common expression, "Don't judge a book by its cover?" What does this useful phrase really mean to you, your life, your friendships, family connections, and school interactions?

Well, this cool story not only shoots the puck to score goals in sports, but it also aims to impart a significant lesson to you as readers, leaders, students, and athletes. It presents a great lesson about the acceptance of others and oneself. It additionally demonstrates the value of determination in our lives as well to achieve what we want in life.

Just how will this bold and brave young boy named Kai show his true potential and steadfast determination in his quest to make the hockey team under a very strict and demanding new coach? How will Salah and Jody also uncover hockey and life happiness as they, too, discover determination and how to excel by accepting others and themselves?

Please know that mistakes are natural for us in life and we learn from them, but assumptions, stereotypes, and hasty judgments are quite dangerous. Getting it wrong the first time is alright, so you don't have to be hard on yourself or ever want to quit. Are you eager to follow along in this entertaining story now about a boy who wasn't accepted onto his hockey team initially during tryouts? He also wrongly judged others as he was falsely judged.

For instance, he labelled the new PE teacher from first sight. He deemed Miss Claire as heartless, odd, and weird after she had chosen everyone to join the hockey team—except Kai. He was so challenged by the coach's rigid demeaning as he likened her to a game or an oddity with his quote, "Yet Miss Claire was like a puzzle that needed solving, and I was eager to unravel her."

In essence, "Get Your Head In The Game: Kai's Hockey Happiness and Lesson in Determination and Acceptance" cleverly highlights how a spirited, focused, and mindful boy discovers the power in never giving up and always seeking and giving second chances in life to others as well as to ourselves. Giving ourselves grace is such a gift and a remarkable skill to possess, as we must also present to others in our lives, schools, families, teams, and communities, too.

It provides a tale of acceptance. Do you know what that character trait truly means? When we accept another person, we embrace and tolerate all that one is. We don't make quick conclusions about him or her. We learn to be totally receptive, open-minded, considerate, loving, empathetic, and compassionate. We can relate to others and be non-judgmental in our actions, words, body language, thoughts, dialogues, etc.

It also delivers a story about feeling included among others, which is something that you'll face not only as a kid, tween, or teen, but also into adulthood as well. It also emphasizes why we must never quit when situations, coaches, teachers, peers, or teammates are different or difficult.

It's time now to lace up. Are you ready to score and soar with a sporty and fun story today? Skate with Kai, Salah, and Jody and keep your eyes peeled for pucks!

It was a dark and foggy night; lightning cracked in the September sky, and thunder crashed outside. I nervously sat by the window pane and created fog by blowing hot air through my mouth onto the window. I could not help but think of how odd Miss Claire had picked everyone to join the hockey team—except me.

To be honest, I judged the new PE teacher as a bit peculiar from first sight. She was kooky and unusual. We made eye contact as soon as I arrived at the hockey field. She stared at me with her deep blue eyes and intense black pupils. It felt as though she was looking right through my soul! Her eyes were glued on me the whole time—she was intimidating and knew it!

"Good day, class!" She curtly greeted everyone.

"Good morning, Miss Claire." The whole class responded, except for me. I was too dumbfounded and scared to respond.

She then strutted straight to where I was standing and threw a hockey puck right toward me. It hurled at me at lightning speed, knocking my senses out for 30 minutes.

The whole class probably laughed at me when I passed out, but at least I wasn't conscious. I woke up at the nurse's office and my friends, Jody and Salah, had sat beside and comforted me.

"Miss Claire said you can't make the hockey team," Salah whispered.

"She didn't give me a chance! Who all made it then?" I asked.

"Everyone, except you," Jody added.

The room was filled with steely silence. How unusual! I knew I wasn't good at sports, but I wasn't as terrible as Joel or Lisa, but they got in! They walked me home in complete silence because I didn't feel like chatting.

Again, I was making fog on the window, a thought popped up in my mind: I sincerely wanted to try and join the team the next day. I was determined to apply my focus on this goal.

The following day arrived because the screeching sound of my alarm clock woke me up, so I popped up, got dressed, prepared to go to school, ate my breakfast, and went to school.

The whole day was quite uneventful—I was just waiting for PE time. I wanted to prove Miss Claire was wrong; she was unfair by picking everyone else and excluding me.

The bell rang and we all headed towards the changing rooms where we changed into our zebra-striped jerseys.

"What most of you lack is confidence!" Miss Claire barked. "Yesterday, I eliminated one of you, but today I'll be cutting two students. I want to create the best hockey team in this whole region," she boldly explained.

Most of the students dropped their heads shamefully.

"This is what I mean: one issue and all of you are ready to quit. To be honest, I want hungry lions on my team, not wimpy gazelles," she insisted.

"And you," she said, pointing at me. "What's your name? And why are you here still after I disqualified you yesterday?" She questioned intensely.

"I want to play!" I tried as much as possible not to stammer or make jerky movements even though I was mortified.

"Alright! I like the fact that you didn't quit. Your determination is inspiring. I'll give you one more chance!" Miss Claire promised.

"I want to see all of you play!" She shouted.

We all sprinted towards the hockey equipment and started playing in a disorganized manner. I immediately notice the disappointment on her sour face, but this was my last chance. I knew I just had to prove that I was a worthy addition to the team.

As soon as I saw the defence slacking, I managed to pass through them. And since the puck was in the perfect scoring position, I sealed the goal. The best part was that the goalkeeper had charged early, allowing me to score effortlessly. My team proudly cheered as the puck swished into the goalpost.

I just wanted to show my potential and steadfast determination. I was so hopeful that it would work out.

Miss Claire blew a whistle, and we huddled around her, paying close attention to what she would say.

"Kai! Good work!" She commended me.

I was thrilled! It was the first step to my hockey success, and I was proud of my achievement.

"Lisa and Joel, you're out!" She bitterly announced as she left.

I still couldn't believe that strict Miss Claire had just congratulated me. My friends, Jody and Salah, came to praise me on that amazing goal.

Yet Miss Claire was like a puzzle that needed solving, and I was eager to unravel her. Even when she started moving her lips, it felt like she had carefully picked her words. In turn, I wanted to know every detail about her—I had never met a person with such a complicated, demanding, and bold personality before. She was totally a mystery and I was planning to solve it while fighting for my rightful spot on the team.

Soon the bell rang, and it was time to go home.

"There's something strange about her," I hinted.

"Who?" Salah asked.

"Who else? Miss Claire!" I told my friends.

"You're just scared of her; like the rest of us but that doesn't mean she's strange!" Salah argued.

"I agree! Miss Claire is definitely a little odd, but I've heard she's an excellent coach. At the last school she used to teach, she successfully led the hockey team to the Nationals and they won!" Jody explained.

"There's still something about her! She changes her mind too fast! One minute she's angry, then the next minute she's okay. She's like a volcano ready to explode at any time!" Kai bellowed.

"Your imagination is wilder than usual! She's just a normal person," Salah insisted.

"There's nothing normal about her!" I kept arguing.

"Okay! What should we do then?" Jody asked.

"We should investigate her. If we find something strange about her, we'll expose her to the whole school," I slyly suggested.

"Alright then, but If you don't find anything kooky about Miss Claire, you owe me a Big Carl's Milkshake!" Salah playfully added.

"Alright then, It's a deal!" I said as I stretched my hand out to her to make a fist bump.

The three of us plotted our plan of sneaking into Miss Claire's house. We stood outside the gate, gazing at the gigantic house as we arrived. Suddenly each of us had second thoughts, but we decided to enter. Inside, the house was cold, and I shivered. It felt as though ice had replaced my spine.

Halfway into the house and mission, we decided to leave since nothing was out place or apparently odd.

As we were leaving, we ran into Miss Claire, who was not as tough as she was at school. She even invited us to into her house and offered tasty snacks.

"Let me guess, you broke into my house because you thought I was too unusual?" She asked.

The three of us were dumbfounded.

"I'm not unusual! I'm just good at my job. I won't report you, but you should never break into someone's house!" She warned. "Now please leave!" She exclaimed.

We could not believe how understanding she was. We were all ashamed of how we had wrongly behaved.

Since that day, I decided to be a better hockey player instead of looking for trouble, judging others swiftly or harshly, and lacking determination for what I wanted.

The next day was quite sunny, and we chose to enjoy it. The previous days had been quite rainy, so I had to take advantage of the excellent weather.

As we arrived at PE class, Miss Claire was already there.

"Get in and next time, don't be late!" Miss Claire warned.

We rushed in, sat, and paid attention to her. She resumed coaching normally. She was pretty pushy, but that was never out of the ordinary. She did not hold the fact that we sneaked into her house or judge us. Instead, she just focused on hockey. Wow, she had such strong determination that I hoped to follow.

Finally, the day ended as eventfully as it had started. The three of us went home together and decided to have a last-minute sleepover at my place, which was fun.

The following few practices were more intense than usual since we were going to a tournament soon. We rarely had time to hang out because of practice. Furthermore, Miss Claire had already chosen the main team, and the three of us were proudly on it.

After lots of waiting and nerves, game day arrived. We showed up at school early. We got on the bus and drove off to the nearby school. We were going to have an intense match, and since it was our first, we had to leave a long-lasting impression. Unfortunately, Salah, who played left-out on the team, missed a crucial goal during the game. The next few days followed him, reliving that moment over and over again. We had indeed left a long-lasting impression, not as winners but as losers.

Miss Claire was disappointed by the results, "You played pathetically!" She barked and left the room. After so much practice, she couldn't help but feel disappointed.

Eventually, she got over it because it was just our first game.

On the other hand, Salah was certainly not over it. He kept wallowing in despair. He kept thinking of the what ifs. Miss Claire noticed this and summoned him to her office.

"I know I played poorly in the game," Salah admitted.

"Why is that?" Miss Claire inquired.

"I was too tense!" Salah answered.

"Which is understandable, but if you keep choosing to pity yourself instead of learning from your mistake, do you think you'll ever improve?" Miss Claire asked.

"Not at all!" Salah answered.

"Enough of the self-pity and give the next game your all!" Miss Claire encouraged him. The team continued its weekly practices since we had an upcoming tournament.

The due day arrived, and we welcomed our opponents at our school. The game started at a low pace, but our confidence started building up, and we began scoring goals.

At one point, it felt as though our opponent's defense started moving in slow motion, giving us ample time to score a final goal. Jody sealed the goal using a reverse flick, earning him a reputation at school. He was assisted by Salah, who had finally redeemed himself.

This victory earned us a chance to go to regionals and eventually nationals, which were our goals despite being a new team.

Our tough coach was well-respected by every school in the country, and we knew she would lead us to the nationals, but it would never be easy. With each passing day, practice got tougher, but we got better, and it was finally the regional playoffs.

The match started, and we began playing as though there was no tomorrow. To move onto the nationals, we had to win regional games. The opponents were outstanding and gave us a hard time, but we eventually won the game by a point.

Our team's next stop was nationals which were two weeks away. At school, there was a celebration since we would finally play in the nationals. It had never happened before.

My friends and I decided to go out the next day to celebrate the victories we had been getting. The following two weeks were very eventful—we had to worry about the finals and the national games. Finally, we did our finals and had to await the results.

The next event was the national games. So we practiced every chance we got because we deeply wanted to win.

The day of the final games arrived, and people from all over the country gathered in the hockey stadium. We had a meeting, and Miss Claire showered us with words of wisdom—it was finally time to bring the trophy home.

The whistle was blown, and the game commenced.

If they thought the previous team was good, this team was way better.

The nationals were the toughest game we had ever played before. Their opponents were too good, and penetrating the defense was tough. They also had excellent passes and dribbled the ball well. We started being super nervous! We had to win, but how?

It was halftime, and we huddled around Miss Claire, hoping to hear words of encouragement, but instead, she was stern and urged us to win the game.

As we returned to play, it was obvious that we grew confident with time, and suddenly the other team started being anxious, and their defense allowed us to score our first goal. Salah passed a sizzling assist that I had to dribble between the opponent's defence and score. The second goal was by Salah, and the third was by Jody, sealing our deal as the champions when the referee blew the whistle.

"Good work, boys!" Miss Claire cheered, her eagle eyes illuminated with excitement.

Learned lessons

As you just read in this sweet tale today, determination is a such key part to success in any sport, lesson, family dynamic, goal, friendship, or objective. Just because something does not automatically work out for you the fast time does not mean you should ever quit or become disheartened.

Just like Kai never gave up despite failing the first tryout, you should always focus and strive harder than before to achieve your goals. Jody and Salah also learned the power of teamwork, acceptance, and friendship in this sensational story, "Get Your Head In The Game: Salah, Kai, and Jody's Hockey Happiness and Lesson in Determination and Acceptance."

Are you now ready to complete some final reflections and free bonus gift activities to apply the outstanding character education and life lessons from sport story? These exercises are perfect for a weekend, a holiday, a rainy or snowy day, a road trip, or any special occasion.

1. Determination Word Splash: Using the example of determination presented in the story by Kai, Salah, and Jody, make a word splash of other terms that mean the same as determination such as focused, persevere, etc. If you are too young to write, read, or spell, them ask a grownup to write for you or use pictures to illustrate. Be creative and colorful!

   _____

   _____

2. Magical Mistakes: As the story showcases, mistakes are natural parts and essential learning lessons in life. Give 2-3 examples of times when you made mistakes and actually magically learned from them. What happened? What did you learn? How did you grow, mature, or change?

   _____

   _____

3. Judge Judy: Who did Kai wrongly judge in this story? Why? How? Discuss with an adult. Have you ever judged anyone too swiftly or falsely? What happened? Explain.

_____

_____

4. Hockey Happiness: Find 2-3 fun facts about hockey the sport, its history, where it is popular or played worldwide, and other trivia. Go online with an adult's permission or check out a book at the local library about this exciting topic.

_____

_____

5. Friendship Card: Design a friendship thank you card for someone special in your life who shows determination and acceptance. Use your imagination and make it crafty or colorful!

_____

_____

CHAPTER 3

"A Boxing Ring of Positivity: Felix and Jonah Knock Out Negativity"

Did anyone ever say you were a downer, a bummer, or a pessimist in life, school, friendships, family events, or sports? Did anyone ever call you a skeptic or a naysayer? Those negative labels infer that you might often act negative, you know. Do you find yourself quite grumpy, negative, and always grumbling each day? Is it normal for you to tend to always be in a bad mood, complain, argue, or say, I can't? It is now time to "check yourself before you wreck yourself," as the popular saying goes.

In contrast, are you currently excited to discover a super, relatable, and sensitive tale follows the lives of two young boys, Felix and Jonah, who dream of becoming future lightweight champions as they gain positivity and optimism along the way? Despite the hardships and obstacles they face both in the ring and out of the sports arena, they always show hard work, maintain a positive outlook on life, and loyally chose each other as friends to achieve their goals. These character traits are a total TKO for success and focus in life!

It's time now to grab your best gloves, your favorite New York hat or hoodie, and take a swing at learning some vital life lessons that will make you smile for miles instead of frown and grimace. "A Boxing Ring of Positivity: Felix and Jonah Knock Out Negativity" will amaze and educate you!

In addition to dodging punches literally in life, in the form of obstacles and setbacks, this engaging tale also reminds us that we can soar and endure with optimism and a positive mindset by our sides. Are you ready to get a great workout for your mind, body, and soul?

In the first place, being positive and having an optimistic outlook on life looks a lot like a smiling face emoji. In other words, it allows you to always look on the bright side of life to notice, cherish, and celebrate all the good things, events, and people. It is close to having an attitude to gratitude and remembering to count your blessings in life, even when you are stressing or struggling.

Being positive or optimistic is a choice that the boys in this story make and it's definitely a daily decision for us as readers as well. We must train our brains to believe you can make good things happen in your life. It means having a can-do attitude toward all life goals, choices, tasks, etc. It also makes finding the lesson in the mistakes or failures and not quitting or blaming yourself when things go wrong.

Besides that, we can battle and win against any negativity or setback when we self-talk and cheer for ourselves. When something good happens, it's always best to give yourself credit for it. Use positive mantras and words each day to uplift and let your mood shift. Plus, it's essential to remind yourself that setbacks and mistakes are temporary. You've got this!

Looking back when they were little, it's obvious that Felix and Jonah have been inseparable since childhood. In other words, they were like two peas in a pod! They grew up in the same tenement in Brooklyn, New York, USA.

Ever since they were young, their peers would swear that their friendship was a match made in heaven. Even though they had different personalities, they understood each other perfectly. They both dreamt of becoming worldwide lightweight boxing champions and would practice together. Each chance they got, they went to practice at the gym together, and each sunrise, they worked up and ran miles to ensure they stayed fit.

The youngsters attended the same school, and even though Felix was struggled in almost all his classes, Jonah helped him and ensured his grades went up. While some of the kids in the neighborhood got into trouble by meddling with the wrong crowd, the duo had big dreams to achieve. Besides exercising and training, they were determined to remain positive, embrace optimism, and only engage with good people.

If you asked the boys about boxing, they would specifically go on for hours about their beloved sport. They even had a scrapbook filled with pictures of their favorite boxing moments and tickets to every match they had attended.

Years passed, and the boys were old enough to fight, and so they decided to sign up for regular tournaments.

One evening, they just could not focus on other thoughts, except for their boxing auditions. They were both excited and anxious. The boys wanted nothing more than finally making their dreams come true so they could move their family to a peaceful part of the city.

In turn, they went to Jonah's house to relax for a while.

"How will you fight?" Felix asked.

"I have a few tricks up my sleeves," Jonah replied.

"I'll show you mine if you show me yours!" Felix said.

The boys went to the garage, sported their gloves, and began their friendly match. Even though the two boys were excellent fighters, they both had different styles. While Felix's tall body allowed him to be the better boxer, Jonah's short and muscular body encouraged him to be the better slugger. Whenever the duo fought, it triggered local watchers to gather around since the fight always got intense.

As they were boxing, Jonah's uncle and cousins gathered around to cheer them on, their eyes glowing with the excitement of watching the duo. Well, until Jonah's mother cut the occasion short.

"Boys! Boys! Enough! It's time for dinner, gather around the table!" She yelled.

Jonah's mother always prepared the best Mexican delights, and the whole family would shower her with praise each time.

"Mrs. Cruz, the meal was delicious!" Felix said as he prepared to go home. "See you tomorrow during our morning run!" He bid his friend goodbye.

The following day the sun rose brightly. Its golden rays flickered across Felix's room, waking him up for his morning run. As he walked toward the door, he could not help but be sad about the situation at home.

Just a week ago, the unthinkable had occurred. The factory where his father worked suffered a devastating fire and had to be shut down. It was not easy for Felix's dad to get another job, so they were finding it hard to cope financially. Felix desperately needed to win the matches to provide for his family. Worried thoughts crowded his mind since there was nothing he wanted more than to help his extended family that lived with them.

So the boys went for their morning run, and Felix went to practice more at the gym. He eagerly hoped he'd be selected soon to fight in a tournament in the upcoming days.

The day went by, and the sun fell away. It was time to audition at the gym. The boys prepared well for the fight and it was finally time to show off their skills.

As they arrived, the man in charge stared at them and laughed hysterically, "You two are way too young to fight!" he argued.

"We have the best skills and the perfect talent," an overconfident Jonah assured.

"Skills and talent? Alright then, show me what you've got." The man demanded.

The boys did not hesitate; both knew exactly what they wanted and were not going to settle for anything less than what they believed they deserved; space and glory in the boxing ring.

After the tryouts, the man in charge, who introduced himself as Rocco, was pleased with the boys' amazing skills. Truly, they were talented, and with the right coach, they would start winning tournaments.

"Alright, you're both in, tomorrow will be the first day, don't be late," Rocco warned.

The boys were pleased with what had happened—it was exactly what they had hoped for. The best part of their friendship was that they were not competitive. Instead, they were collaborative and co-operation; they did not want to outdo each other and just wanted to succeed together.

As they walked home, they went to the gym to practice more and later arrived at their respective houses. As Felix reached home, he was saddened by the conditions that welcomed him: his family did not have money to buy food that night, so they went to sleep hungry.

If only I'd gone to Jonah's house, maybe I'd get some of the tasty tamales that Mrs Cruz always prepared!

The next morning was worse— the landlord had given them a three days notice to vacate the premises if they could not deliver the rent.

Since Felix liked to keep everything to himself, he did not tell his best friend, Jonah, for fear of worrying his buddy.

The boys went to school and decided to practice at the gym before anyone arrived. The session eased Felix's mind; working out always relieved his stress.

"I can tell you've been worried. Is everything alright at home?" Jonah inquired.

"Yes, nothing too crazy. Everything will be fine within no time," Felix stammered.

"Are you sure? I've noticed you've been more tired than usual. Did you eat breakfast?" Jonah asked.

"Yes! I already told you everything at home is alright," Felix insisted, but Jonah was his best friend and always could tell when Felix wasn't being truthful.

Before Jonah could elaborate, Felix left the room and went to shower, so he could join his classes.

After school, the boys went home, and as they arrived at their tenement, they were shocked to see all the furniture from Felix's apartment thrown out, and his family sat outside helplessly.

"What happened? Mama? Papa?" Felix asked, voicing his concern.

Where would they live? When would the horrible situation end?

He was utterly distraught.

"Honey, I've borrowed some money from Jonah's mother. It's just enough to find a cheaper place," Felix's father explained.

Jonah assured his friend that everything would be alright and no matter where Felix moved, he'd always be there for him, and they'd be lifelong friends. Felix and his family eventually settled in a rusty trailer in Buffalo, New York, USA.

This situation made him feel worse than before—he had to find a way, and he had to locate a solution as soon as possible, or else his siblings would fall into the wrong crowd.

From that day, Felix never missed boxing practice. He was always on time and left the gym later than everyone else. He only had time for two things; school and boxing.

"I don't see you as often anymore!" Jonah insisted. "I know. It's just that since we moved, I haven't had the time to hang out," Felix explained.

"I understand, but would you like to hang out like the old times?" Jonah asked. "Sure!" Felix replied.

The two boys were like brothers; and regardless of the time they spent apart, whenever they reunited it always felt like there was no time spent apart.

That evening, they fooled around with a few jabs in the air and eventually had a friendly match which Felix won. It was just like the old times, but this time, it was evident that Felix had grown stronger and was now the best fighter despite their different fighting styles.

At first, it did not really bother Jonah; besides, without Felix to push him to work out or go on morning runs, he was falling behind. He even started wondering if he still wanted to be a light-weight champion, but after having the conversation with his pal, his perspective was crystal clear once again.

They both decided to meet at school early in the morning, just like in old times, and practice harder than the rest. After school, they trained at the boxing ring.

A year passed, and the boys turned 16. Felix was getting better with each passing day, and even though Jonah tried to reach his full potential, his journey was slower.

Due to Felix's skills, Rocco agreed to be his coach, and the two began practising more and more each day. After a few practices, it was clear that Felix was ready for his first tournament.

"Congratulations hermano!" Jonah cheered. "You deserve this opportunity more than anyone," he added.

The boys hugged one another. Even though one of them was going to start their career before the other, their deal was to cheer for each other.

Felix eventually improved every chance he got. He didn't want his first tournament to be his last.

Finally, the due day arrived, and it was time for the match. An audience gathered around to watch the tournament. Jonah came earlier than everyone else to show his undying support for his friend whom he considered a brother.

The match ended in a victory—Felix's first triumph! He then used the money he won to help his family.

Jonah started shining as well and even though his career's growth was slow, he did not lose hope until he was also selected for his first tournament which he won. He embraced positive thinking, optimism, and a growth mindset. He also remembered to use positive self-talk.

Years passed and after a series of eliminations, the duo had been informed that they would have to fight each other in the future championship games.

"Hermano, let's make a deal," Jonah proposed.

"I hear you loud and clear, my brother," Felix replied.

"Whoever wins will take care of the other one's family," Jonah said.

"It's a deal!" The boys sealed their deal with a fist bump.

The days in training were slow, but the date they had been waiting for finally arrived. They talked about the match and sealed their deal once again.

The match started very seriously as both players were adorned in their fighting gear. Felix did not think twice. He came in fast and threw a punch, which he missed. Jonah lashed out with a straight left, also missing.

During the first half, the pair kept missing—it was as though they didn't want to hit each other.

The second half was quite eventful. The fight began and Jonah threw in a punch and missed, giving Felix the chance to slip in a counter attack, sending mild chills through Jonah's body. The fight took such a long time but there was no progress. Even though Felix punched Jonah, it was clear that Felix didn't want to fight his buddy.

As a result, the match ended in a draw and they shared their money in half, changing the lives of their loved ones. They learned the value of mutual respect, positive thinking, and optimism.

Learned lessons

As this amazing tale clearly demonstrated in this theme and life lesson today, we must always remember that some friends are worth more than anything. In fact, they are like family to us since their support and love will always bring out the best in us and inspire us to be the best that we can be!

Likewise, this story encourages us to choose them all the time, just like Felix and Jonah, who always had each other's backs, as far as in boxing, friendships, loyalty, character education, and life! This terrific tale is a total TKO as it highlights key lessons like mutual respect, team work, friendship, loyalty, positive thinking, and optimism, so it's now your turn to enter the ring! Let's pause now and take an educational punch at some final reflections and free bonus gift activities to practice the life lessons from this fun story:

1. BFFs: Recall the two friends' names from the story. How are they similar? How are they different? Cite examples from the story to justify.

   _____

   _____

2. Word Up: Define positivity and optimism in your own words. Use context clues from the story to create your own definitions. You may also write or sketch what these words mean to you or use them in original sentences.

   _____

   _____

3. City Slickers: Recall two American cities and the setting's state from this story. Locate these places on a map.

   _____

   _____

4. Life Lesson: Summarize what the story's ending reveals about life lessons. What was your aha moment after reading this book or main takeaway? Explain.

   _____

   _____

5. Box Talk: Identify 2-3 boxing terms or vocabulary words from the story. What do they mean? Use context clues for hints.

_____

_____

CHAPTER 4

"Spin Your Wheels: James Embraces The Power of Practice and Self–Belief"

Even if your beginning isn't smooth, you shouldn't ever give up in life, at a sporting goal, on any academic task, regarding a social skill, making a dream a reality, or concerning anything else that you want to master for yourself. If there's a strong seed planted in your heart to master something, then you can water the seed with practice, be confident, and make it bloom.

Likewise, this excellent story follows a young boy named James, who didn't know how to cycle well or confidently at first. Therefore, fear paralyzed and froze him.

While James was extremely gifted, witty, and a natural academic scholar due to his critical thinking and intelligence, he wasn't an athletic type automatically. Some people are born with innate talent for biking, but this wasn't the case for James, who was a late starter or in the sport.

In particular, James lacked self-belief at first and the know-how to spin his wheels to success in the biking sport in the beginning stages as he felt fearful, anxious, embarrassed, dismissive and unsure. However, he later became the best cyclist by choosing to believe he could do it, listening to his parents' advice, and discovering the magic of practicing regularly.

Why is practice powerful? How is it similar to pumping gar in one's car or air in one's bike tires? Well, practice means rehearsing over and over again. It makes trying to perfect one's skill until he or she masters it completely. All athletes train, practice, and condition, so you'll need to add it to your sports, school, or hobby menu. Gain a solid understanding of how and why practice is so integral by reading this special story!

In addition to practice, "Spin Your Wheels: James Embraces The Power of Practice and Self-Belief" further explains what self-belief is and why it's so closely linked to goal achievement, sporting success, and triumph in any school, life, or social contexts. When you believe in yourself, you showcase a can-do attitude. If you think it, you can achieve it. If you believe it, you can become it! This is almost like gripping the handle bars on a bicycle tightly since you reinforce that you're then in total control over the bike and that you're proceeding onward with self-belief and confidence.

Are you eager to bask in a lovely mother/father/son relationship that's also depicted in this fantastic tale to highlight the value of patience, having a support system, the benefits of practice, and the gift of self-belief?

Beyond that, this heartfelt story also cautions us against having too much pride and fear of failure in life that act as broken brakes. Fear, doubt, and lack of self-belief will hold us back in life from any dreams, goals, aspirations, or desires.

Are you ready to spin your wheels with James in this uplifting tale today? Pump some air in your reading tires and let's go now for a glorious ride!

The bicycle wobbled as James peddled. His father held the bicycle firmly so he wouldn't fall.

"Hold tight, my son!" His father puffed.

"I'll fall!" James screeched.

"Easy, James! You're doing well," His father insisted as he slowly let go of the bicycle and James steadily rode on his own unknowingly.

"Dad—you can let go now!" James shouted. Of course, he didn't know that he was riding smoothly on his own.

"You're on your own, James. Keep going!" He cheered. Suddenly, the realization that he was on his own made James anxious.

"I'll fall, Dad. What should I do?" He wailed.

"Press the brakes!" His father yelled as he rushed towards him.

Dad eventually caught up to him, but it was too late. James was unable to press the breaks, leading him to crash to the ground.

"Where were you, dad?" James asked in a shaky voice, suggesting he was about to cry.

"Are you hurt?" His father asked since he was extremely concerned.

James stormed out, unable to be pacified by his father. James then rushed to the house to tell his mother what had happened.

"Mother! Mother! Dad let go of the Bicycle and I fell!" He wailed.

Although James was not hurt, he was still shaken by the event.

"Oh, my love! That's how you learn how to ride a bicycle by falling and getting back on the bicycle," Mother calmly explained.

"But mom—" Before he finished complaining, his mother offered him a piece of pie and he forgot about the biking ordeal.

Since he was a toddler, James was always an overly cautious child. He carefully thought about everything he did and avoided taking risks. That's why cycling made him uneasy at first. He associated falling with failure; and through analysing everything properly, he was able to succeed at most things even at a young age—except sports.

James was blessed with sharp wits. His grades were the highest in class and he was able to satisfy his parents with his academic achievements. However, when it came to sports, he was just mediocre. Sports just didn't feel natural to James as they did for many of his sporty peers.

First, he tried to play soccer, but he couldn't score goals. He then dabbled with track running, but he was extremely slow like a snail. Next, he considered basketball, but he was too short. Finally, he even took a turn at boxing, but he was too weak.

His parents understood the importance of having an active child—it would be beneficial to his health, and so they tried to teach him various sports until he found something he was passionate about.

His father once took him to play baseball, but it was unsuccessful. He even enrolled him in figure skating, but James kept falling.

With cycling, it was different since he was able to ride for a few seconds alone which gave his father a tiny glimpse of hope.

The next day, his father took him to ride the bicycle, but this time James mastered the courage and self-belief. He did not show outbursts even after falling as James remembered that his mother told him that to learn cycling patiently. Dad also advised how James had to fall a couple of times to master it before applying the magical tip of practicing.

After a few practices, James became a skilled cyclist and eventually fell in love with riding his bicycle. His confident radiated as he pedalled down the street. He went everywhere with it; to school, to the shops, to the playground, to the beach—everywhere!

He became so passionate about riding his bike and his parents felt so proud of him because that is all they ever wanted.

As the days went by, it was clear that James was cycling faster than ever before.

"Have you noticed that our son is a really good cyclist?" His father asked his wife.

"What's on your mind?" His mother responded.

"He can possibly join a cycling competition—there's a good chance he can win!" His father explained excitedly.

"Well, I think that's a great idea!" His mother agreed.

After having their discussion, that night during dinner, they brought up the subject.

"James?" His mother called him.

"Yes, mother?" He replied.

"We're so happy that you found a sport you like and engage in every single day," she emphasized.

"We think you're incredibly talented and you might have a chance of winning cycling competitions," his father joyfully added.

Once his father explained, James started laughing hysterically. "I'm just a plain kid who rides his bike. There's nothing special about me, unlike those professionals who have dedicated most of their lives to training. I'm already at a disadvantage as a late starter," he giggled.

"We can see it in you! You have real talent," his mother pleaded.

James was very enthusiastic about cycling, but the thought of losing held him back and froze any self-belief in him. "I appreciate that you guys believe that I can win, but frankly I don't believe that," James murmured in a gloomy voice.

Deep down James was disappointed by the fact that he did not even try, but he was too prideful and could not let his parents know how he truly felt. He genuinely wanted to participate, but he lacked any trace of self-belief that he was a true 'athlete' unlike other kids who had an edge over different sports.

"Think about it, James. You've mastered with practice and now cycling is your domain. You just have to start by believing in yourself as much as we believe in you!" Mother insisted as she walked away.

The sun fell away and rested, allowing darkness to cover the land. The stars twinkled brightly in the pitch black sky. He went to his balcony and watched them, still deep in thought. How could I let my insecurities get to me?

After trying to see things from a different point of view, he finally decided to attempt it. He first took small steps in gaining self-belief.

The next day he woke up at the break of dawn, got on his bicycle, leaned forward in his seat, and began pedaling as fast as he could.

Suddenly, it became a routine that he had to do each morning. He noticed that not only did riding his bike every morning increase his confidence and polish his skills, but it also gave him peace of mind and an immense sense of self-belief. Within no time he started to believe that he had the potential to win the competitions he was to sign up for.

After cycling practice, he decided to discuss his decision with his parents during breakfast. The dining room was filled with delicious aromas. Furthermore, he was starving after practicing so early in the morning.

"We noticed you have a new routine," his mother noted.

"I can tell that nothing ever passes you!" James chuckled.

"So, my son, what have you decided?" His father asked.

"I'll be joining the competition, but I'll take it to step by step with tons of practice and self-belief. There's no need to rush the process and even though I feel comfortable while cycling, I still have a long way to go," James explained.

His parents were thrilled with the news, so they rushed to hug him.

"Folks, step by step," James emphasized.

"Alright, step by step!" His parents agreed.

The very next week, James confidently went to the cycling tryouts at school and was selected for the inter-house cycling competition. He practiced harder than he had ever before because he wanted a chance to represent his school on a regional level.

The due day arrived and the cyclists lined up, awaiting the signal to go off.

"The first person to cross the yellow line will win an opportunity to represent the school at a regional level," confirmed the coach. "One, two, tree," he continued as the signal blasted, making the cyclists pedal as fast as they could.

Each of the contestants hoped to win the opportunity and so they gave it their all. This time, however, James was unable to win. He came in at a close second, making him feel disappointed at his loss.

"I told you! I'm not an athlete, but you had to push me!" He barked remorsefully.

"It was your first competition, so cut yourself some slack! You were amazing," his mother consoled him. "This is what life's all about. If you want to feel content, you should always choose to engage in things that make you leave your comfort zone, force you to practice, and gain self-belief! This was alright and you were pretty good!" his mother added as she patted him on the shoulder.

The duo even biked to their favorite ice cream shop and enjoyed their evening together. Even though he didn't win, James decided that he wouldn't feel sorry for himself. So he decided to practice harder, but this time enlisting the help of his father, parting ways with his pride because what he wanted was growth.

Every morning, before the sun adorned earth with her golden rays, James would wake up to practice with his father as his coach. He would start by doing warm-ups and leg workouts to ensure his legs were strong enough to pedal as fast as possible. Afterward, he would cycle and his father would count the amount of time it took him to reach from one end to the next.

Shortly after, he began seeing results and decided to sign up for a cycling competition based on his surge of self-belief. Unlike the other one, this wasn't a school competition. The prize of the winner was a chunk of money and a shiny medal.

James kept on practicing with the help of his father and it was undeniable that he got better with each passing day.

"Son, your energy is as bright as the stars. You can achieve anything you want!"

His mother reminded him often to sharpen his mindset, increase his self-belief, and to get rid of his self-doubts because she knew that his son's biggest setback was his low esteem.

The next few days saw James training harder but he never complained. He was grateful that he had a purpose that wasn't just studying like he had been doing since he was in elementary school. Furthermore, cycling gave him opportunities that he never had before and allowed him to make new friends which he was new to him as a introvert.

Lastly, the day of the competition arrived and James was driven to the venue by his father who supported him every step of the way and encouraged him to enjoy himself since the journey was a meaningful time for every successful athlete—it was the defining moment.

The venue was bustling with a lot of activities. His mother stood on the side to watch him and his father helped him wear his cycling clothes while giving him helpful tips on how to win.

At last, the whistle blew and the cyclists pumped as fast as they could. James was one of the first few, but he had a tough time passing an opponent who was pedaling for all he was worth.

Suddenly, he moved to the front and it was just him and that opponent. James tried to match the guy's energy, but it proved to be impossible since he was cycling like there was no tomorrow. This speed was probably not a good idea because his energy was bound to get depleted quickly, but he didn't seem to get tired.

On the contrary, he was advancing towards the finish line with each passing second.

Janes realized that he was pitted with this machine of an opponent who rode his bicycle as though he was a lightning bolt.

Regardless, James didn't give up because he yearned for his first victory and decided that he would also give his opponent a tough time beating him. He remembered what his father had told him, put in the work, and realized that he was getting closer and closer to his opponent.

They were both approaching the finish line and James was conscious of nothing except winning the competition. He filled his mind with the thought of the glory his victory would bring, so he cycled faster than before. For how long he'd been cycling—he didn't know but what he realized was that he'd be crowned the coveted victor on that special day.

He proudly overtook his opponent and crossed the finish line.

At this point he hadn't yet realized that he had won, because he was still basking in his element. He was shortly brought back to reality by the chants of the onlookers. He was also able to catch a glimpse of his parents' beaming faces.

Since he was the victor, he was given a medal and money, making this one of the best days of his life. Although it was just the start of his cycling career, he didn't care because now he had proven to himself that determination, practice, and self-belief were the recipes for success.

Learned lessons

If you want to become good at something, this story highlighted how you should change your mindset and work hard. Determination, self-belief, and practice all bring success. As James proved with his biking win and growth, faith, practice, and confidence can all truly move mountains!

If pride, uncertainty, doubt, or anxiety ever grips you in your pursuit of a goal or a dream, as fear paralyzed and froze James, just know that self-belief and practice will serve as your fuel to triumph. Just like pumping gar in one's car or air in one's bike tires, practice means rehearsing over and over again. It encourages us to keep trying repeatedly to perfect one's skill until we master it.

"Spin Your Wheels: James Embraces The Power of Practice and Self-Belief" further taught us what self-belief is and why it's so closely aligned to goal achievement, sporting success, and mastery in any school, life, or social contexts. When you fully believe in yourself, you exude a can-do attitude. Similar to gripping the handle bars on a bicycle tightly, self-belief lets you seize full control over the bike and your targeted goal as you cruise with confidence, like James did.

Are you ready to spin your wheels with James in this uplifting tale today? Pump some air in your reading tires and let's go now for a glorious free bonus/gift ride! Now it's your turn to put the pedal to the metal and try some final reflections and free bonus gift activities. Practice as you apply the amazing character and cool life lessons from the story:

1. Practice Pledge: Make a pledge or a vow today to commit to practicing a sport, a skill, a language, or any goal. Write it down to hold yourself accountable. Visually post it somewhere to remind you to practice. Recite it aloud with speech practice as well, maybe in front of a mirror.

   _____

   _____

2. Word Wiz: Define practice in your own words. You can also use a dictionary or go online for the term with an adult's permission. Then use the word in an original sentence or draw what it means.

   _____

3. Bike Blitz: Research some of the most famous cyclists in the world by going online with a grownup's permission or checking out a book from the local library. Pick 2-3 of them to discuss. Holler for history, research, reading, and sports!

4. Movie Madness: Name 2-3 movies, books, songs, or TV shows that affirm the theme of self-belief as James and his parents vividly expressed in this story.

5. Practice Performance: Write a letter, create a song, make a story, or perform a puppet show to teach a vital life lesson about casting your pride aside or the importance of practice in sports and in life. Apply the character traits and lessons from this story as you devise your message creatively.

CHAPTER 5

"Sing With Ian The Ice King: Breaking the Ice With Creativity and Confidence"

Are you ready for a royally good read today, one that's memorable, relevant, and moving? Do you need to add a new favorite literary piece among your current home library collection? Even if your environment or current circumstances feel more like a peasant's than a king's or queen's right now, this educational story is perfect to reiterate the vital life lessons that you should never abandon your dreams, hopes, desires, or goals.

Likewise, pause for a moment here to state your goals for the day, week, month, or year, as our main character will mindfully manifest and model for us throughout this story.

With a pure heart, creativity, confidence, determined goals, empathy, and compassion for others, and a competitive approach, you, too, can make your dream life in school, sports, friendship, or aspirations a reality, just as Ian showed us. It's a power packed story with suspense, emotion, humor, and lots of character education lessons, morals, and socioemotional takeways. It also affirms how we can use our parents, friends, relatives, coaches, and community members as resources.

Are you set to get bolder in Boulder with Ian in this fun but frigid adventure? He'll surely lead with love and logic as he models how to gain power, self-belief, accountability, and ownership for his figure skating goals. By displaying a can-do attitude, giving 100% of yourself, and fully immersing and dedicating yourself to your goals, you can go for gold in life as well!

Ian's nonstop efforts enable him to never give up. He keeps his eyes on the prize by working and practicing hard and clearly believing in himself.

What's more, you'll also acquire some winter and skating-related vocabulary words from the story as well as some historical knowledge in the form of two iconic figure skating legends mentioned in the tale. Ian will show friendship and impress you with his loyalty, compassion, and empathy toward others.

In sum, this tender tale travels to the Rocky Mountains in gorgeous Boulder, Colorado, USA. It follows a friendly, upbeat, male figure skater named Ian who yearns to win the championship games as soon as possible because figure skaters typically retire at a young age. However, a pandemic strikes, making his athletic life and dreams feel stuck.

He's also challenged as a young male in a sport that is often deemed as feminine and dominated by girls. Can Ian eventually pave the way for his dreams? How will he break gender barriers to achieve success? What role will creativity and confidence play as he tries to break the ice and enter this competitive world with glory and self-belief? Who will assist him along the way? How can he combat stereotypes?

Let's lace up a pair of skaters, sport some gloves, find your cozy boots or snowshoes, and don a scarf, as we make some magical music and "Sing With Ian The Ice King" today. We'll uncover how being imaginative, thinking outside the box, and innovative can foster your own creativity and confidence as well.

In a chilly but lovely winter wonderland in Boulder, Colorado, USA, where the shimmering snowflakes fell softly on the ground, covering the land in a blanket of snow most of the year round. There lived a special boy called Ian. He was the best skater in his neighborhood.

Everyone admired his strength and speed. Hockey scouts would flock to his father's compound in attempts to recruit Ian for ice hockey, but he only had one dream; to be a professional figure ice skater. He wanted to combine his love for music and skating into one!

He tried ballet before he dreamt of being a figure skater; The Prince role in The Nutcracker fit him so perfectly since he was not only muscular but also graceful, unlike other boys in his class who were quite clumsy. Afterward, he decided to be a figure skater; he wanted to be an athlete who changed the world for the better and to prove that boys could skate and still be masculine.

So, every morning, he'd wake up to practice at the ice skating arena in town where the ice sparkled like glass. He twirled and spun on the crystal ice skating arena. His skills were so good that passersby would forget what they were doing and watch Ian in awe. Hus talent was as clear as crystal and he fought hard to be seen for who he truly was, despite some gender obstacles about males in the sport. Ian treasured his talent and capabilities.

His mother; Angelina, was a famous ballerina. Her shows were one of a kind. She was able to do Swan Lake as both main characters; the Black and White Swan; interchanging roles effortlessly. Her achievements were Ian's main inspiration, although he was overlooked due to being a boy.

Every morning, Ian still woke up early and went to the skating arena to practice harder than before. He was able to follow in his mother's footsteps, since he was a quick learner and a creative soul. Every move he made in the arena came from his heart. Ian rarely copied other people's moves, unlike other artists.

From a young age, skating interested Ian. He fell in love with the clumps of white snow that were scattered on the ground. Being in the snow made Ian truly feel at home, like a true ice king!

Every so often, his friends would accompany Ian to the skating arena since he adored snowy winter days. He cherished his pals who skated too, but they weren't half as good as Ian was.

Naturally, he never stopped trying to be a great figure skater. He yearned for glory and all he ever wanted to be was a star like Scott Hamilton and other male pioneers in the sport. Throughout childhood, he idolized the famous Olympians and learnt their every move since he wanted to be just as victorious and confident someday.

Since his mother saw Ian's steadfast efforts, she hired a group of coaches to help him win a future Olympic gold medal. Each time Ian went home from school, he'd find a group waiting to coach him at the gate; and despite being frustrated by the amount of work he had to do and the creativity that Ian had to cultivate, he clearly understood he had to practice to achieve the greatness he yearned for.

Accordingly, the city of Boulder loved Ian due to her upbeat personality and wanted the best for him since they saw how hardworking he was. Ian pushed herself more than most people and was kind to everyone.

As seasons passed, his skills got better and everyone in the town started calling Ian the "Ice King" because his talent was unmatched.

Even though he was one of the youngest male figure ice skaters in town, he was creative and confident.

Also, most boys admired him and wanted to be like Ian because of his determined and outgoing personality. Since he was a child, he also was passionate about the stars and watched them every night, thinking about the future that he hoped would be great.

Suddenly, Ian's father passed away when he was still a young age and this amazing dad had instilled creative ways of expressing oneself in Ian's mind. So each night, he remembered how Father used to say, "If you want your dreams to come true, you need to befriend the stars, so they can grant you a wish."

In turn, every night, he'd sit outside, look at the stars, and make a wish, "I wish to become the best figure ice skater in the whole region," he politely exclaimed.

"I'd love to shine bright on the ice just like you do in the night," he sang.

Once he uttered this, a bright star twinkled in the pitch-black sky.

After practicing in the skating arena with his coach of the day, Ian went back home.

To keep his father's dream alive, the following night he'd sit at her window, admiring the stars, and politely whisper, "I wish to become the best figure ice skater in the whole world!"

Just then, the largest star twinkled once again. Slowly by slowly, it became a habit, and every single night, Ian went to see the stars to ask them to grant his wish after practicing on the ice.

Despite his efforts, he still believed that the Universe was alive and that he had to attract his dreams through good deeds, creativity, and confidence.

Years passed, and his skills were sharpened. Every night, after practicing, he asked the stars to grant his ultimate wish. All he wanted was to manifest his divine purpose and align his destiny with the Universe.

After a few years of working hard, he signed up for the World Figure Skating Olympics, which he eventually auditioned for and got in! Everyone in the town was super proud.

Ian was always kind and always tried her best to be creative; that's why the whole town adored and wanted him to achieve his goals. His heart was truly made of gold just like his father's heart; Ian's heartfelt intentions were always clear from the start; he never tried to fool anyone. Instead, he uplifted others.

Whenever he went back to town, the children and the elderly were all excited since he tried his best to cheer them up. Indeed, Ian's dream commenced way before he even signed up for the Olympics because he knew that a true ice king deeply cared about others.

In fact, Ian's level of understanding was unmatched—even when he trained with other skaters, he did not have a jealous spirit.

Ian helped all peers whenever he could because he understood that winners aren't scared of giving.

But, sometimes, the nicest people go through unkind situations, even though they deserve all the goodness the world can give. Once he was accepted as a competitor at the figure skating Olympics, a terrible disease began spreading all over the world. Ian had to leave Boulder, USA to go to the Olympics. Yet due to the disease, it was impossible.

All these events made Ian anxious, as he wondered how he'd achieve his dreams when figure ice skaters typically retired at a young age.

His mother came to pick Ian up and they went back to their hometown. When Ian arrived, he couldn't believe her eyes. The disease had spread all over the city.

Everyone was suffering. Furthermore, he was stuck at home and couldn't understand what was happening; all he wanted was to go ice skating in France.

Regardless of the state of the world, he didn't give up. All his adversities made him Stronger, despite life falling apart. Even though life had been halted, he still tried to be a better figure ice skater by working hard creatively and constantly—he didn't know how he'd ignite his dreams, but he knew he'd achieve them.

Every day, he'd race outside and skate on the ice like there was no tomorrow. His passionate nature brought hope that everything would go back to normal and random people started recording and posting him on social media since they found his art amusing and relaxing.

Each time he skated on the ice near home, he'd trend on social media and this increased his reach—making people ask who he was. His talent had become a remedy to relieve stress during hard times and even though others didn't know who he was, he kept pushing harder because all he wanted was art to soothe other people's distress.

On a pitch black night when the stars shined brightly, giving light to passers-by, he sat on her balcony and wondered what to do. He wanted to change the world but felt as though all efforts weren't big enough. Ian felt so powerless, so he decided to express his emotions through ice skating.

Every time he practiced, someone would record and post, and the video would go viral. Even though people were stuck at home, by figure skating, Ian was able to ease their minds for a while. He soon became a public figure, despite people lacking any idea of who he was or what her name was—Ian didn't care, though. All he wanted was to be known for whathe did and whether people knew him or not didn't bother creative and confident Ian.

Years passed and the pandemic subsided thanks to a hardworking group of doctors and the competition was revived. News of going to France to participate in the World Figure

Skating Olympics filled his heart with joy. Finally, he'd be able to fight to achieve the dreams that had stuck with Ian all this time.

He was accompanied to France by his mother and they checked into their hotel. The day of the competition arrived and the arena was filled with people. Other participants danced beautifully and were ranked by the judges. The highest mark was 8 and since Ian was the last participant, he had to skate in a way that was unique compared to all opponents.

His costume was white and he wore a crown that was adorned with crystals. He started skating slowly and as the music got intense, his movements got faster. Ian spun 345 times per minute which was higher than Kaori Sakamato, seizing his crown as the figure skater with the highest number of rotations per minute. Once he finished skating, the judges were surprised by Ian's performance, giving him the highest score and crowning him as the victor.

Shortly after, he started trending on social media as the boy who skated on the ice during the pandemic. His fans recognized and applauded for Ian being a beacon of hope to the world at such a tough time.

Learned lessons

Does that wintery and wonderful tale now make you want to sip hot cocoa, warm your frigid hands by a fire, and nap a bit? It was so amazing to discover the story's main theme that even when things are seemingly impossible, you shouldn't lose hope. With creativity and confidence, things will eventually fall in place just like in Ian's figure skating dream situation; he was able to win a trophy since he chose to never give up, exude a competitive mindset, be compassionate and empathetic toward others, and break the ice with creativity and confidence.

"Sing With Ian The Ice King: Breaking the Ice With Creativity and Confidence" was a heart-warming tale to reinforce why we need to embrace a pure heart, creativity, confidence, determined goals, and a competitive mindset as we strive to make our dreams, goals, aspirations, hopes, and objectives in life in school, sports, friendship, or aspirations a reality!

As you recall Ian's path to success, please remember the major role that creativity and confidence played as he entered this sport's highly competitive world, broke gender barriers as a male, and led himself to triumph, fame, and glory as well as gaining self-belief.

Always try to use imaginative, thinking outside the box, and innovative thinking to foster creativity and confidence in sports and all other areas of your own life.

1. Bolder in Boulder: Name the American state where Ian resided in this stellar story. Then locate it on a map and then go online with an adult's permission and locate 2-3 fun facts about the state flower, flag, weather, industries, or other information.

   _____

   _____

2. Confidence: Using each letter in the word, confidence, create an acrostic poem to reflect what the new term and character trait means to you. For example,

- Creating power and

- Ownership for our dreams.

- Never allowing fear to win.

- Finding a can-do attitude.

- Insisting on giving 100% and

- Dedicating yourself to your goals.

- Endless efforts to achieve them,

- Not ever giving up.

- Clearly believing in oneself and

- Eternally empowered that your dreams will become a reality!

3. Legends: Identify two figure skating legends mentioned in the story. With an adult's permission, go online and research 2-3 fun facts about both of them. You may also check out biographies or autobiographies about these figures from your local library.

_____

_____

4. Skate Great: List 2-3 skating terms, equipment, or jargon used in this book. Practice grammar by stating which parts of speech they represent.

_____

5. Friend Till The End: How did Ian show friendship, compassion, and empathy toward others? Give 2-3 examples.

_____

_____

The second part of the stories

CHAPTER 6

"Mateo's Bull's Eye of Bravery: The Grit Not To Quit"

Just because you're shy, short, quiet, weak, different, unsure, or clumsy, doesn't mean that you can't achieve your own unique dreams, specific goals, big objectives, and strong desires. Whether you want to become a star athlete, a scientist, a pilot, a firefighter, a lawyer, a plumber, or an archer, this sensational story will teach you that all dreams are truly within your reach when you learn and apply life's essential character traits.

What are these important character traits, you may first wonder? Well, this brilliant story is packed with powerful growth mindset lessons to give you a big boost of confidence, the necessary social skills, a positive pep talk, a bold blast of motivation, and the key steps to think, act, transform, feel, and excel like a hero!

In turn, "Mateo's Bull's Eye of Bravery: The Grit Not To Quit" introduces you to a shy and clumsy, but brave and determined boy who battles for his lifelong dream and passion in archery. He acquires how to increase confidence, stay focused, practice with persistence, and rock with resilience over the course of the tale.

Now it's time to grab some sunscreen, your water bottle, a cool hat, and your favorite sunglasses because we're visiting the arid and amazing New Mexico, USA, where Mateo dreams of archery. But please watch out for cacti, coyotes, roadrunners, and other Sonoran Desert obstacles along the path as you discover what it truly means to gain the grit not to quit.

So what's grit, you may ask? Is it the rough, scratchy, and tough texture of the desert sand? Well, like gritty sand that can withstand dangerous weather, high temperatures, and other immense challenges, grit refers to having a positive, growth mindset; it encourages us to have a confident attitude of never quitting or ever giving up on what you really want to achieve or do in life. Are there any musicians, rappers, or poets out there reading this? You can easily remember grit as "not to quit" because it rhymes!

Next, let's follow along and take our aim at mindful motivation with Mateo as he patiently learns how to hit more than a bull's eye when it comes to perseverance, resilience, grit, confidence, bravery, practice, active listening, and courage. Besides, he also gains a better understanding of how to rock with resilience.

Like grit, resilience is also a positive mindset where you mindfully use persistence, perseverance, and focus; in essence, it's your ability to bounce back and stay strong as you channel your inner hero and refuse to become defeated, negative, or ready to quit.

Have you ever been constantly told you weren't good enough or didn't look like the other typical athletes in your chosen sport? That's exactly how Mateo initially felt at archery due to his weak arms, shy stance, anxiety, fear, and overall awkward demeanor,

How does Mateo eventually discover the grit not to quit and how to rock with resilience in both archery and life? Who supports Mateo when he considers giving up? Let's find out, friends/amigos! Vamonos!

It all begins with our determined desert dude, Mateo, in the majestic state of New Mexico, where the Sonoran Desert sand stretches like a radiant rainbow. From age two to now at age twelve, this shy boy, often called a wallflower, immediately fell in love with archery. He even made his own bows and arrows from household items and things in nature, so he could practice his sport daily. Yearning to become an expert, he later read all the books, studied manuals, reviewed videos, and watched exciting movies about knights, dragons, and archery. He was mesmerized and focused on giving archery his best shot.

"Mateo! What did I tell you about making those homemade bows and arrows? You're way too small, weak, and unsteady for such a rough and tough sport!" His mother, Rosa, would yell, but he would sprint away with his cherished bows and arrows, clutching them like gold.

"Don't worry. He'll soon learn the grit not to quit!" He's small, but he's definitely my strong-willed son!" His father, Maximo, would reply as he patiently tried to model proper form with Mateo using their beloved family's bow and arrow, a treasured heirloom.

"Max, your shy son is a drowning duckling when it comes to anything physical! Why doesn't he just keep his nose in the books and study to become a doctor? He's all brains and no brawns," Mama protested.

"Honey, he's perfect just the way he is," Dad replied as he gave Mateo a gentle pat on the back. The two grinned gleefully while watching Mama roll her eyes.

As Mateo grew older, he became more and more fascinated by bows and arrows. He yearned to hunt animals and earn an expert marksman award like his gifted father, famous archer grandfather, talented cousins, and successful, sporty uncles as they earned shiny medals after medals every weekend in Taos, Albuquerque, and other major cities' archery tournaments,

Ultimately, Mateo decided to ask for his own real bow for his 12th birthday. He then enrolled in after school classes. But instead of feeling encouraged by his buff coach, Mateo felt so puny, doomed, and awkward; like a tiny guppy in a pond with gigantic sharks! The other students giggled each time Mateo struggled to find the proper stance or even pull the bow and arrows accurately with all his might due to his small size.

Still dreaming to become a modern Robin Hood or a New Mexican Thor, Mateo later joined his amazing family in their weekly archery practices. However, Mateo always missed the bull's eye, clumsily slipped on a rock or a hole in the ground, sloppily shot at leaves on trees instead of the bull's eyes, and typically began shaking and sweating from nerves, fear, and dread. He never seemed to fit in as the others perfectly hit their marks with grace, speed, precision, ease, confidence, and accuracy.

In turn, Mateo eventually stopped attending archery classes and even those family practices. He sadly hid in his room, tearfully watching the others from his bedroom window as they perfectly nailed their targets like rockets launching into space.

"My son! You should go to the library, sit, read, and just study about archery since you're way too small and weak to actually do it," Mama argued.

"Nonsense! My son can do anything that makes him happy. Mateo has my full support!" Papa insisted, making Mama as red in the face as the chili peppers in her tasty recipes.

As the days passed, it was clear that Mateo aimed to become the best archer in the whole of New Mexico. But how would that be since he was more like a baby deer than a hunter as far as full of nerves, lack of confidence, body weakness, and clumsy feet?

Such thoughts somersaulted through Mateo's mind and made him feel defeated, but the next day, he'd wake up with a smile, ready to conquer his archery dreams.

On a fateful day, as he was walking to the bus stop, he spotted a poster:

ARCHERY COMPETITION! YOU MUST BE 12 YEARS AND ABOVE TO JOIN!

Without thinking twice, he signed up for the competition, and during the next few days, he practiced nonstop. The only thing that raced through his mind was winning the competition, and at times, he'd forget to eat even his favorite arroz con pollo because he was too busy practising.

Meanwhile, Christian, his older brother, was also a top archer in New Mexico. They shared toys when they were little, but he was his role model, and he was coming to town to watch Mateo.

"You shouldn't have called Christian! It's a waste of time," Mama complained.

"Mateo will be competing for the first time, so he deserves our full support," Papa added.

You know I don't support this! He should've chosen a sport that requires only brains, not brawn and brains!" Mama huffed.

As a result, Mateo crouched by the staircase, hearing his parents arguing. Mama was never supportive ever since he was young. She always tried to make Mateo forget his dream of being an archer, which made him super sad. Mateo's father, however, was always by his side and guided him throughout his journey. He showed him all his tricks so he could impress the judges.

Since it was their first lesson, Papa taught the five rules of archery. But Mateo lacked confidence due to his tiny arms and shaking knees. However, Papa told Mateo about a magic secret, the grit not to quit. Because Mateo was as smart as well as a great listener, he practiced daily and adhered to every trick that Papa showed during each and every shooting practice.

The next lesson involved the steps of archery. Papa taught Mateo how to make clean shots that would guarantee a victory. At the end of each lesson, Papa would always give Mateo an assignment in which he'd always succeed in.

After days passed by, Christian arrived in town. "I heard you want to be like me, little bro," he giggled.

"I want to be better than you—the best in the country!" Mateo proudly replied. His newfound confidence was one of the qualities a lot of locals thought was unique since it wasn't fake. Even though he didn't master something the first time, Mateo discovered how to hold his head high and took time to focus, persevere, think positively, and improve until he perfected it.

"Alright! Show me what you've got!" Christian challenged.

Mateo strolled to the simple archery stand built by his father to practice firmly holding the bow and releasing the arrow, which directly nailed the bullseye.

"Impressive!" He cheered. "But have you seen this trick?" Christian asked as he released five bows that landed precisely on the bullseye. The trick greatly impressed Mateo so much that he couldn't stop begging his brother to teach it throughout dinner.

Then he volunteered to help Mateo practice for the upcoming competition the next day. "You need to amaze the judges! They must see a true archer despite you being a newbie!" Christian urged.

"Being a newbie? Does that matter?" Mateo asked.

"My dear hermano, don't you know if you win, you'll be the youngest archer in New Mexico to do so?" he asked.

"I didn't know that!" Mateo replied.

"You've got the grit not to quit, bro! If you win and continue winning, not only will you earn medals and the glory of the people of New Mexico, but you'll also change history," Christian explained.

"Change history?" Mateo truly couldn't believe what his brother was saying.

"Oh please! Don't fill the sensitive boy's head with silly nonsense! Here, go to Mama Nacho's shop and bring me two burritos," Mama bellowed.

In times like this, Mateo wondered whether his mother truly loved and believed in him like she did with Christian. As he strolled to the shop, thoughts clouded Mateo's mind, and he couldn't think of one thing at a time.

That night, he couldn't sleep. Proving Mama wrong while changing history seemed like the perfect plan.

The days went by quickly, and it was the eve of the main archery event.

At the break of dawn, Mateo eagerly awoke to practice. Christian also woke up and helped him practice. But Mateo's muffled mind was somewhere else.

"Where has your mind wandered off to? You need to focus!" Christian advised

For a while, they practiced well until it was time to rest.

"It's been a great practice, but I need some time to relax," Mateo exclaimed.

"Yes! Please go and eat breakfast," Christian encouraged.

The duo decided to rest. Mateo had a few hours left to prepare, but since it would be his first competition, he wanted to give it his best and leave a mark on people's minds. So their practices grew more intense as the due day inched closer.

The following day, Mateo anxiously went to the shooting range alone to test his skills.

Christian was behind Mateo, watching silently, and as soon as he finished showing new skills, they heard someone clap.

"Oh please! Again with that? Why are you filling your baby brother's mind with nonsense!" Mama yelled from the kitchen.

Mama wanted a shy, genius, bookworm son who would only do things like read, study, and enter quiz competitions. As much as Mateo tried to do all these things—it wasn't enough for Mama; all she saw were flaws whenever he shot his arrow.

Ever since he was young, Mama tried signing Mateo up for test prep classes, but the teacher said he lacked the memorization skills. She tried signing enrolling him in art, but the art teacher said Mateo wasn't neat or creative enough. She even tried steering him toward pottery class, but his hands were too shaky. Instead, he almost broke every pot during class, prompting the teacher to kick him out.

Mateo gave it his all, but it was simply never enough. He understood that he had to find something he was passionate about, and that was archery. Yet he knew that he had to apply resilience, grit, and perseverance to succeed.

On the other hand, Papa had always been supportive throughout Mateo's journey, but Mama was never happy. Instead, she valued the opinions of the women at the Spelling Bee who would bad-mouth Mateo for not behaving like a bookworm since he wore glasses, was small, and looked similar to a young genius.

The next day he would prove Mama that he was indeed good enough just the way he was, despite the resentment he had received throughout her childhood.

The night before, he couldn't sleep a wink! He was excited and anxious at the same time. The trick Christian had helped to prepare was simply otherworldly. The audience would definitely be in awe!

Finally, the big day arrived. The sun blessed the earth with its bright light, making the desert utterly beautiful. Everyone in town arrived at the field. Papa and Christian were also there, and they waved at Mateo. The only person who was missing was Mama. Even though he didn't want anyone to know—the situation saddened Mateo.

The judges arrived, and his opponents began shooting on the range. Some were good! Others were terrible and made the judges chuckle hysterically. But no archer exhibited a mind-blowing trick that landed on the bullseye.

The past few days were filled with hard work, dedication, grit the not to quit, and lots of practice. Papa showed him what to do every step of the way. With Papa and Christian by his side, Mateo applied his grit not to quit and found a wonderful level of freedom he'd never felt before—it was both shocking and adventurous. They supported everything he did, and that made Mateo happy and proud. He then remembered everything he was taught and planned to make the crowd wonder.

Mateo mindfully prepared for the competition. He practiced positive self-talk and deep breathing. He sported a comfortable out-fit and wore his beloved bow around his shoulder. He held his arrows steadily and confidently waited his turn.

Hs time finally arrived, and as Mateo proudly walked on the field to the shooting range, he saw Mama walk to her seat near Papa's. This made him happy, and Mateo planned to give a performance of a lifetime-with grit and grace.

"Good gracious! It's going to be a wonderful show!" Christian exclaimed. "That's my brilliant bro!" he kept chanting.

You can do this, Mateo! Show them what you're made of! Glow and grow with grit not to quit" Papa added.

"Mat! Mat! Mat!" The two started chanting together.

"Ready!" Mateo said as he removed his bow from her shoulder and held it steadily with his arrow.

Before the whistle blew, he confidently and patiently added four arrows to his bow, making people wonder. Suddenly, all eyes were on Mateo, and the arena went silent as the audience waited patiently to see what would happen.

Finally, he gazed into Mama's eyes, and when the whistle blew, he released the arrows which hit the bullseye, making the audience roar. They'd never seen anything like this before! The small, shy boy in front of them was now simply bold and brilliant.

He eventually retired to his seat to await the results. The head judge walked to the podium and announced the first and second runner's up, but Mateo wasn't among them. Just when he was about to lose hope, he was announced as the winner of the competition for showing a unique trick.

The crowd cheered as Mateo walked to the podium to accept his medal. He was also commended for being the youngest to chase his dreams, no matter what.

At home, there was a feast! Everyone was invited, and the women who often badmouthed Mateo now praised him. This ordeal made Mama think of the times she'd been unsupportive toward Mateo simply because she wanted to change the opinions of women who weren't worth it. She went to him, apologized to Mateo for treating him poorly throughout the years, and promised to help him to achieve his dream of changing history and becoming the youngest archer in New Mexico.

The whole family embraced and enjoyed the wonderful evening. The next few days were filled with a lot of practice since Mateo would soon compete in his next tournament. He received the unconditional support of all his family members and won. As he kept excelling competitions, they grew tougher because he faced some of the most skilled archers. Yet his grit not to quit, resilience, and determination were unmatched and brought him joy, pride, and success. Eventually, he was recognized by the whole state as the youngest archer to ever secure the tournament.

When he reached the national competition, he had to prove his title was well-deserved. His journey to being the best archer in New Mexico was soon cut short when he won the national title and then proceeded to global competitions. All in all, this brave boy beamed with the grit not to quit. He was now the best archer in the world!

Learned lessons

Like mindful and mighty Mateo in this uplifting story of family support, strength, self-confidence, and stamina, how can you show the grit not to quit in your own selected sport, hobby, future career path, goal, objective, or dream today? Using perseverance, motivation, a positive attitude, and rocking with resilience, just remember that you, too, can be whoever and whatever you want to be; and you can play whichever sport you want to enjoy, as Mateo proudly proved.

In fact, don't ever let your appearance, weight, strength, ability, race, class, or any other factor stop your own unique dreams, specific goals, big objectives, and strong desires. It's vital to believe that all dreams are truly within your reach when you learn and apply life's essential character traits that Mateo displayed. By embracing a positive growth mindset, constantly practicing, finding support from a trusted family member, coach, teacher, or friend, and showing your grit not to quit, you can strike your own Bull's Eye of Bravery!

As a result of this story, you're now ready to increase your confidence, stay focused on your goals, practice with patience, power, and persistence, and rock with resilience at whatever sport, objective, or dream you desire!

Based on this story's valuable lessons, please never feel like you aren't strong, good, or worthy enough just because you might not look like the other typical athletes in your chosen sport. You shouldn't allow yourself to be trapped by other people's shallow opinions or rigid expectations of you. Always aim to please yourself first, not others.

Here are some final reflections and free bonus gift activities to apply the character and life lessons from the story:

1. Grit Not To Quit: When did you ever show grit in your life? How did it empower you and make you feel like a hero? When can you apply grit to your chosen hobby, sport, career, or goals in the future? Give examples.

   _____

   _____

2. Vibe With Your Tribe: Recall two people who always supported Mateo's dreams. How did they offer assistance?

Likewise, name two positive people in your own life who also provide constant love, support, and patience to you.

_____

_____

3. Grit Goal: Complete this sentence: I'll gladly use grit today in order to improve at my sport by

_____

_____

4. Grit Group: Identify someone from your friend or family group who models grit and resilience so well. Talk to this person about helping you to improve your skills.

_____

_____

5. Math Matters: Scan the story again and count the number of times that the author mentions grit.

_____

_____

CHAPTER 7

"Carl Can: Optimism and Positive Beliefs In Ourselves Make Us Stealth"

Have you ever heard the popular expression that it's better to fill your own cup up first before pouring into others' glasses? Well, this useful life saying also applies to friendships, family relationships, school, sports, self-confidence, optimism, positive thinking, and self-belief. These character traits will enable you to float freely, mindfully, and successfully through life.

In other words, unsupportive friends should never make you feel like you can't ever achieve your life goals, dreams, desires, or objectives. They should never serve as roadblocks on the happy, healthy and hopeful highway to fulfilling your sporting, academic, extracurricular, and lifelong dreams, goals, and aspirations.

Likewise, this gripping story truly makes a splash as it follows a young but creative boy, Carl, who's very gifted at the sport of swimming, extremely smart, and very sensitive. But when he needs the support of his friend, Carl doesn't get it. Instead, Carl initially feels more like a daring, dynamic dolphin surrounded by groups of angry, hungry orcas.

As a result of the story's inspiration life lessons, Carl eventually learns about how to become his own BFF, motivate himself mindfully, and how to serve as his own support system. As you grow up, it's also essential to recognize who your true friends are, but it's also vital that you discover and use your own empowering character traits: optimism and belief in oneself. Just as the story's title strongly suggests, "Carl Can: Positive Beliefs In Ourselves Make Us Stealth!"

So are you ready to get stealth with positive beliefs in oneself today? Now let's find our goggles, swim trunks, and beach towel as we prepare to deeply dive in and discover how to gain positive beliefs in oneself, a keen sense of optimism, and steps to become one's own BFF or support system. This story will use Carl as a mirror to demonstrate how you can swim gracefully and strongly against the tides, turmoil, struggles, and weary waves of life!

So what's a positive belief in oneself, you may ponder? Like a life vest when you're just learning to swim or doggie paddle at first as a novice, thinking positively and having full faith in yourself can keep you afloat when the waters are rough? Optimism is a cheerful growth mindset; it's a "can do," proactive, positive attitude that endows you with confidence, perseverance, and resilience, so you'll never give up or quit on what you really want to achieve or do in sports, school, friendship, or life.

Again, if there are any musicians, rappers, or poets out there reading this, you can easily remember the affirmation, Optimism and Positive Beliefs In Ourselves Make Us Stealth, since it rhymes! Word up to you all!

Now let's use our best breaststrokes, strongest backstrokes, and paddle positively with Carl as he masters optimism, positive belief in oneself, how to be one's own BFF and support system, perseverance, confidence, bravery, practice, mindfulness, and resilience.

We'll journey to Florida, home of Mickey, Minnie, and Carl for some fun in the sun!

One spring day in a sparkling public pool in sunny Florida, USA, two friends were debating as they apply their own sunscreen. "I think it's a great idea," praised Carl.

"I believe the idea is so lame!" replied Jerry.

"I know I can do it!" Carl insisted.

"You're already at a major disadvantage!" Jerry argued.

"Say what? What disadvantage?" Carl asked, facing Jerry, looking at him straight in the eye.

"Well, the swimming team is already full of prodigies who have trained their whole lives!" Jerry explained.

"I can start training too!" Jerry exclaimed.

Carl literally felt like a fish out of water and couldn't believe that instead of his best friend encouraging him, Jerry was actually discouraging Carl toward a dream that he deeply wanted to make a reality.

The swimming gala was to be held the next day. The coach had to pick the best swimmer who would eventually win the medal, making the school proud.

While the meeting was in progress, Carl sat at the back and paid attention silently.

"Tomas is the best swimmer, but some of you have to volunteer as subs. We can't depend on him. God forbid in case of an emergency, then we'll be doomed!" Coach warned apprehensively.

The room froze with silence—no one dared to utter a word until a coin from Carl's pocket fell on the ground, making a loud noise and turning heads.

"Who are you?" The coach asked. "I've never seen you before!" He continued.

Carl stood up, cleared his throat and announced, "You need a clear strategy in order to win!"

"Son, I don't think you understood my question. Who are you?" Coach asked with a stern voice.

"My name is Carl and I can finalize the approach for the next day's competition to make it easy for Tom," he kindly offered.

"Alright Carl, thank you. Why don't you go ahead and give the team and I the chance to finish our meeting? The earliest opening to join the team isn't until next year." Coach revealed.

"But…" Before a shocked Carl could complete his sentence, Coach barked, "NOW!" This order prompted a nervous Carl to exit the room immediately.

Disappointed, Carl thought, if only I'd listen and think positively…

The next day was the swimming gala. Carl woke up early and attended school. The pool area was filled with workers preparing for the big day, so he stood and watched with a gloom of sadness. Suddenly an interesting idea popped up in his mind: How can I show the team that optimism and positive beliefs in ourselves make us stealth?

Carl sincerely wanted to help, but the last time he tried to pitch in his ideas, Coach kicked him out—but with good reason, since Carl wasn't part of the team, and so he didn't hold it against the coach. So he sat and waited for all the team members to arrive.

"Hey Carl! How have you been!" Jerry walked towards him.

I've been a busy bee!" Carl giggled.

"Busy? With what?" Jerry curiously asked.

"I want to join the swimming team," Carl excitedly exclaimed.

"I still think it's very lame," Jerry taunted him.

Noticing the tension in the air, Carl left without saying a word and went to look for the swimming team.

"Carl, dude! Did you just leave me hanging?" Jerry voiced, but Carl disappeared without saying a single word.

Next, Carl entered to Coach's office and found him trying to make calls but was only met with a beep. It turns out that Tom, the best swimmer at school, didn't report to school today because he had Covid.

"I can stand in for Tom," Carl offered confidently.

"You, again?" Coach grumbled.

"Yes, I can do it," Carl protested.

"Alright then, kid, wear your suit and meet me at the pool area," Coach advised.

Suddenly, Carl stood still quietly.

"You wanted me to give you a chance and now you're chickening out?" Coach asked in an angry voice.

"It's just, I didn't think you'd say yes so, I didn't bring my swim trunks!" Carl explained.

"Kid, if you want to be a great athlete—you must always be prepared," Coach voiced. "You can find a new one in the changing room," he added.

All at once, Carl raced towards the changing room and changed. He then ensured that he glued the swimming cap to his scalp and securely wrapped his goggles around his eyes. He looked like a human version of Nemo!

Without thinking twice, he ran towards the pool area and dived in. Chlorine filled his lungs, and the echoing sound of the water splashing as he swam as fast as he could towards the next end.

After a short while, he was already on the other side. Coach was in complete shock! Carl was brilliant—he was positive, focused, motivated, and mindful indeed! Furthermore, since Tom wouldn't make it, Coach knew that Carl would be the perfect substitute.

"Kid! You're in. Meeting in the next 5 minutes," Coach confirmed as Carl still floated in the water.

On the other hand, Carl was now overwhelmed by a wave of big emotions. His plan had finally worked! Yet what shocked him was how his first trial landed him his first competition!

He exited the freezing water and changed back to his school uniform. Afterwards, he went to the meeting. He figured that the meeting was to finalize the last few gala details.

"I've made an important decision since you're all aware that Tom came in with Covid and won't be joining us today," Coach explained. The rest of the team's eyes were glued on the coach and paid attention to every word he said.

"Who will be the substitute?" Joanna interrupted, genuinely showing concern for the fate of the team.

"Carl will be the substitute!" Coach swiftly answered.

"Carl? Who's Carl? Is he even on the Swimming team?" A concerned Dave asked.

"Yes, he's starting today! This kid can teach us all about positive belief in oneself to become stealth!" Coach smiled and proudly answered.

The room was filled with murmurs. They couldn't understand why a new member would represent them during such an important event.

"I know how difficult this might be, but Carl is brilliant, self-motivated, mindful, patient, and optimistic. He has a major chance of winning the competition," Coach insisted.

So Carl sat quietly until the coach called upon him to introduce himself.

"Hi! I'm Carl, I was in the meeting yesterday. As I was walking around the pool today, I noticed something that can give us an upper hand," he said.

Suddenly the room was silent as everyone was eager to hear what he had to say. "The depth of the pool is perfect for me to propel faster and defeat the opponents," he naively added.

"That's the mystery? You don't have a strategy? Coach, why would you put the fate of our team in this amateur's hands?" Joanna asked in a voice suggesting she was highly irritated like a sting ray.

"My strategy is winning based on applying life lessons and character traits of optimism, self-belief, confidence, and becoming your own BFF and support system," Carl cheerfully added.

"I understand he's still a newbie and clearly, he's never practiced a day in his life but I saw his capabilities. You'll see that I'm right," Coach emphasized.

Next, the other teams started to arrive and prepare for the competition. Carl started doing warmups, and the coach offered him helpful tips to win the gala.

Finally, it was time to compete. The swimmers lined up on the corner of the pool. The whistle was blown, and all the swimmers dived in and swam at the speed of light. During the first round, Carl came in fourth. His teammates began gloating.

In the next round, he came in second, and during the last three matches, he earned first, increasing his points tremendously. Even though he didn't win the competition, he was the first runner up, which had never been achieved before at his school, making everyone cheer and celebrate the victory.

However, Jerry wasn't happy with his friend's win, so he didn't talk to him during the holidays—it was clear he was a jealous friend who wanted to deter his friend's dreams, and when it didn't work, jeering Jerry became angry and gave Carl the silent treatment instead of cheering him on.

During the holidays, Carl stayed in shape to give his best during swimming.

The holidays ended, and it was time to go back to school. Carl was soon summoned by Coach, who advised him that if Carl wanted to succeed, he had to go to a school that offered a special swimming program, so he applied.

At school, he entered more competitions and won many medals for some time since he followed Coach's strategies. His teammates also grew fond of Carl and admired his leadership.

As the days passed, Carl waited for a response, but nothing came up. Just when he was about to give up, something interesting happened! He was amazed! Finally, he'd be able to work towards his goal as the best swimmer.

"Mom! Dad! I got in the program!" He rushed into the house excitedly.

"We're so proud of you, son!" His parents assured Carl.

That night, Carl couldn't sleep an inch. It felt like he was floating in a whirlpool of bubbles.

The following day arrived pretty quickly. He woke up and prepared for his first day.

Just when he was heading towards the bus station, Carl heard someone walk behind him, but each time he looked behind, he couldn't see anyone.

Suddenly, he felt someone hit him behind, prompting him to fall to the ground. The person started kicking his hand until he couldn't move it.

Carl had to be rushed to the hospital. He thought he'd never swim again, but to his shock, he was fine and only had to take some time off to rest.

"Did you recognize who hurt you?" The police asked him. But Carl didn't have any vivid memories of the bullying ordeal.

Over the next few days, Carl got better quickly and went to his dream school, where he was received warmly. The feeling was out of this world. He would finally be able to train with the best, so he would become the best.

As Carl was being shown around, he marvelled at the sight! The pool area was what impressed him the most. It was huge and deep, like something from the summer Olympics! While it was a haven for him, it would be awful for anyone with a phobia of deep waters.

He couldn't wait to start practice the next day. But again, that night he couldn't sleep. He thought that he might never swim again due to his injury, but that was far from the truth because, at this specific moment, his dreams were slowly becoming a reality.

Carl soon fell asleep, and the next day, he was woken up by the chiming of bells. He quickly went to the pool and dived for his morning swim, which refreshed him.

The swimming team was exactly what he dreamt of, but he was disappointed since even though he was the best at his school, the coach put him on the bench since he wasn't the best at his new school. He had to prove to his coach and teammates that he deserved to be part of the main swimming team who got the chance to compete.

Every day, he woke up earlier than the rest and pushed himself more than anyone else in the team. At first, no one cared that he worked harder, but since he started swimming faster than most of the swimmers in the first team, he was eventually added due to his undying devotion to swimming.

Afterwards, he started going to swimming competitions that were harder to win than in his former school because most swimmers were skilled. This didn't make him wallow; instead, he worked harder, applied lessons of self-belief, optimism, and confidence and started winning a few competitions with health and stealth!

His former coach used to come to watch all his competitions and showered him with kind words, so Carl kept pushing himself positively and mindfully.

During a certain tournament, he noticed that his former friend, Jerry, was in the audience. As soon as Carl saw him, he remembered the beating and bullying he had suffered, as the painful memories gushed back to him.

Once the competition ended, Carl was crowned the winner, and Jerry walked toward him.

"I know it was you, but I'll forgive you for it!" Carl whispered as he walked away from Jerry, who stood perplexed, unable to move.

Jerry was soon arrested and locked up in juvenile detention.

Carl kept working harder to achieve his dream until he was selected to represent his country in a worldwide tournament. Proudly donning a gold medal around his neck on the podium, Carl eventually won, solidifying the fact that his dreams were now a reality.

Learned lessons

Just like Carl, life will certainly toss you many toxic tidal waves in the form of obstacles, bullies, challenges, twists, turns, and naysayers. Yet you shouldn't let fake friends ever get to you, deter you from your goals, or ruin your positive vibe. Instead, you should always do what you want and apply character traits of "Carl Can: Optimism and Positive Beliefs In Ourselves Make Us Stealth."

Always embrace the mantra that it's better to fill your own cup up first before pouring into others' glasses, like Carl displayed. When approaching friendships, remember to swim upstream with self-confidence, optimism, positive thinking, and self-belief. These lifesaving character traits will serve as your new superpowers as float freely, mindfully, and successfully and gleefully toward your goals in life, school, sports, and friendship.

Bullies never win and unsupportive friends should never make you feel like you can't ever achieve what you want in life. If you truly yearn to make a splash, emulate our resilient, creative, courageous, Carl, as he eventually mastered how to become his own BFF, motivate himself mindfully, and how to serve as his own support system.

As you mature, be sure to clearly recognize who your true friends are and pour from your own cup first and foremost. Go for the gold, like Carl did, with optimism and positive belief in oneself. The story's title echoed," Carl Can: Positive Beliefs In Ourselves Make Us Stealth." Now it's your turn to dive deeply to get stealth with positive beliefs in oneself now. Here are some final reflections and free bonus gift activities to apply the amazing character and cool life lessons from the story:

1. Carl Can: Review the story again and list 2-3 ways that Carl showed a "can do" attitude or mindset toward swimming, friendship, and life. Discuss some examples.

_____

_____

2. Stealth Health: Recall a time in your own life when you used positive thinking, self-belief, and optimism to overcome an obstacle or deal with a difficult person. Give examples.

_____

_____

3. No Bull at Home or School: Recall the bully or antagonist from today's story. How did this person act like a bully? How did this person's words and actions impact Carl?

_____

_____

4. Be Your Own BFF Goal: Complete this sentence: I'll become my own BFF and support system today in order to improve at my sport by

_____

_____

5. Pour From Your Own Cup First: With a grownup's permission, find a non-breakable cup. Fill it with positive words and ideas to motivate you when you face a challenge in life.

_____

_____

CHAPTER 8

"Saleem's Mindful Miracle: Persevere With-out Fear"

Do you believe in miracles? Are you an avid fan of learning new skills and life lessons to increase your own confidence, performance, focus, motivation, and sports swag? Have you presently been struggling with fear, anxiety, lack of confidence, or self-doubt lately in school, family, friendships, sports, or life in general? Are you seeking some practical tips to triumph successfully over fear and nerves in all your endeavors? Is it time to discover how to persevere without fear?

While this superb story doesn't contain any genie in a bottle characters, any special potions, capes, or any wonderful magic wands, it does present a terrific tale and some mindful, resilient, effective, and transformative life lessons about a determined, relatable young boy from Detroit named Saleem. He dreams of becoming the best soccer player in the world, despite his special challenges related to his vision and his overwhelming fears and anxiety.

After engaging in this inspirational story, you'll soon score loads of points and new character traits to better empower and motivate you mindfully after discovering Saleem's strong and sporty spirit of never quitting enables him to power through and persevere until he becomes victorious in the end. Ready, set, go for the goal!

Stretch out those muscles, lace up those running shoes, chug some water to hydrate, and build socioemotional stamina with this tenacious tale today. In essence, "Saleem's Mindful Miracle: Persevere Without Fear" will swiftly transform your own chances of winning in life, sports, school, or friendships. Use your special needs as a superpower, not a super sinker!

Do you have a special need, a challenge, or a weakness that often feels like you're constantly playing defensively in life? Are you easily frazzled, full of fear, or prone to giving up when addressing goals, dreams, tasks, sports, objectives, or desires?

Accordingly, this heartfelt story will freeze your fears as you acquire what perseverance means and how to apply it to your life. Grab your equipment and sprint to the reading (and soccer!) practice field with savvy, smart, and sweet Saleem as he uncovers how to increase his confidence, combat his fears, and shed his self-doubts to win big in his preferred sport. Don't worry, we won't make you do drills, pushups, or situps

Did you hear that whistle blow? It's now turn to turn up and examine what it means to persevere without fear. If you're curious what persevere really entails, it refers to a positive, proactive, steady, and consistent mindset that keeps you set on the right track to persist toward your goal and not quit. Think of it like knee pads or a helmet in sports since perseverance has a protective role for us.

Have you ever felt like you weren't the ideal or perfect model of what a member of your sports team should like or act like? Do you constantly feel like you aren't good enough? Take some tips from Detroit, Michigan, USA's Saleem as he gains wisdom and practices perseverance in the game of life and soccer.

Looking back, it was a bright summer day in Detroit, Michigan, USA. The sun illuminated the sky with crimsons, making the Lake Michigan glitter like diamonds. The day was warm, and the tides were low. It was the butterfly migration season, and everyone made their way to the shore to watch them fly away.

Detroit was also home to a bubbly boy called Saleem. Ever since birth, the stars aligned and every so often he dreamt of being the best soccer player in the world.

"Mama! Mama! I learned how to do Cristiano's Elastico!" Saleem skipped to his mother each time he learned something new.

"Papa! Papa! I discovered how to dribble like Neymar!" He rushed excitedly to describe the tricks he learned vividly.

Saleem's parents supported his soccer dreams and always encouraged him to practice harder to achieve his goals. He deeply loved to play soccer at Lake Michigan, so every evening, he would make his way to the shore and play with the local boys.

How can a boy with poor eyesight and thick glasses ever excel at soccer? They stared at Saleem with wonder.

Instead of concentrating on the negativity, he kept pushing harder, hoping one day he'd achieve his delightful dreams.

He performed just like any other player on the field, wearing his sports glasses with protective lenses, and an elastic band to hold them in place, always fearing that this special need would derail his soccer success. In the end, he was able to score points for his team during the local tournament.

Once the game was over, he went to the shore and began to think about his future. He watched the sunset, little children playing in the water, the boats sailing, and the older soccer stars perfecting their craft. None of them had eyeglasses! Saleem noticed.

All these observations made him feel anxious. He desperately wanted to achieve his dreams and decided to work harder towards his goals, despite being born with impaired and weak vision.

As Saleem went back home that evening, he asked Mom more about soccer and even mentioned the topic of possibly getting contact lenses.

"Mom, will I be the best soccer player in the world despite my weak eyes?" Saleem asked politely.

"Why not? You can do anything and as long as you have the will to achieve your goals and you learn to persevere without fear, my sweet son. The Universe will bless you," Mom replied while tucking her future soccer star into his cozy bed.

"The team members laugh at me whenever I play with them," he explained.

"You're a special player, honey. They should be glad you're on their team, scoring all the goals for them!" Mom insisted.

Saleem was pleased with his mother's responses, so he decided to try harder to achieve his dreams. While he was fearful of asking his mom about contacts since he had no idea how those slimy, slippery little circles would fit into his eyes and stay there, he knew that he had to persevere without fear.

"Do you think you can call the eye doctor ASAP and schedule me for a contact lens fitting?" Salma asked politely.

"Yes! I fully support you. I'll call in the morning and also show you how easy it is to use contact since I use them myself for yoga and swimming," Mom gladly replied while she kissed his forehead.

She then turned off the lights and tiptoed quietly out the door like a mouse.

"I'll become the best soccer player in the world!" He declared as he closed his tired eyes.

The next day arrived and as soon as he finished eating his delicious breakfast, he made his way to Mom's car to visit the eye doctor. He was shaking and sweating because he had never tried to wear contact lenses before.

Upon arrival to the office, all the staff members were so nice to Saleem. The eye doctor was a patient man who examined Saleem's eyes and confirmed that he was a perfect candidate for contact lenses.

After watching the technician, Mr. Omar, and Mom show Saleem how to insert contacts, Saleem soon began by trying to place them gently into his eye one at a time. While he kept dropping them at first, he remembered the lesson to persevere without fear. It only took two or three more tries before Saleem inserted and removed his contacts successfully and even giggled at how easy the process truly was.

The technician, Mr. Omar, cheered him. "You can make a big difference and persevere without fear if you believe in yourself, show patience, and practice, practice, practice." It turns out that Omar was a retired soccer coach before moving to America.

Saleem sat still in silence. All he wanted was to get better as each day passed by. His monkey mind bounced ever so often; his dreams seemed too good to achieve, but he kept faith and was confident in himself to freeze the fears and summon the cheers!

"To become the best, you have to learn your strengths and weaknesses," Mr. Omar added.

"Do you think I can be the best of the best?" Saleem asked, as he dribbled the ball.

"Yes, you totally can!" Mr. Omar encouraged.

Saleem practiced for a while until the sun fell away and rested for a while. He couldn't sleep soundly that night. All he could think about was achieving his soccer dreams, forgetting to have fun during the process.

The following day the sun rose and shone brightly, casting golden rays through his bedroom window, waking Saleem up to get ready for school.

Saleem sat like he was stuck in quicksand, glued to the bed, a little bit scared. It was his first day at school, and even though it was entirely normal to feel a little bit nervous, he couldn't help but also feel embarrassed by these roller coaster emotions as he stared at his contact lens case.

"Keep your head up, Saleem! Your dreams are valid, have faith in yourself." Mom uttered.

"Yes, Mom!" He replied.

Saleem gobbled his breakfast, and his mother drove him to school. It was a new year, and he decided to join the school's soccer team despite his special need.

Even though he was brave, he was still scared of changes but his fear wasn't as strong as his determination to achieve his dreams. So he kept his head up and mastered how to persevere without fear.

There was a color explosion at school, the kids were different and embraced their diversity. While Saleem wasn't as talkative as Oscar or as clumsy as Alberto, he was the most talented soccer player in school. All he wanted was to win a scholarship to join the famous Soccer Academy of Seattle, Washington.

That evening after classes, he went to the lake to practice. While he was doing warm-ups—he couldn't help but hear footprints behind him.

It was Mr. Omar!

"Pass the ball to me!" He instructed.

When Saleem passed the ball, the old man gripped it with his feet and dribbled non-stop, making the passers-by stop and stare at his incredible skills.

"Soccer is an art, my dear friend, so you have to master it!" He said.

"Can you teach me that?" Saleem begged.

"Yes, of course, but you have to be here every evening to practice! And you also need to apply the special trick: learn to persevere without fear…" The old man insisted.

The next day was an important step in Saleem's upcoming soccer career.

He was going to try to join the Soccer Team. He arrived early at school and raced across the field to warm up. He started to practice the impressive move that he would show the coach. The technique was difficult yet it seemed simple—but with the correct power, timing, and angle, he would make the perfect shot.

Later on, other members of the team started arriving. The boys began bullying Saleem. "Shouldn't you be dusting off your glasses on the bench?" Rico barked.

Yet Saleem was too busy trying to make the perfect shot, so he ignored him; this angered Rico, so he grabbed Saleem's ball, walked straight to him holding it in his hand, and looked straight in Saleem's brown eyes. Fear froze Saleem as did anxiety, but his contacts stayed firmly in place.

"New dude! Didn't you hear what I asked? Are you deaf and blind?" He asked. The other boys started laughing hysterically but instead of being rude, Saleem paused, took a few deep breathes, tugged the ball from his hand, and kept playing.

Shortly after, the coach arrived and it was time for the tryouts. The boys began showing their moves and since the coach didn't prioritize Saleem because he was a knew. Saleem had to show his cool tricks last.

Once his time arrived, he focused and breathed deeply to freeze fear, remembering what the old man had said. Saleem kicked the ball powerfully, making the perfect shot that went straight into the net—-the coach added him to the team despite doubting his abilities.

His time with the team was unbearable! Other teammates treated Saleem like he wasn't part of the. team.

"Hey, water boy! When will you stop?" Rico asked as Saleem was running around four cones, warming up for a friendly match.

As usual, Saleem ignored him and this only made him angrier—Rico wondered why he never talked back and crafted a cruel plan to get Saleem to leave the team.

The friendly match was Saleem's first tournament with the team and he wanted to give his best performance. During the game, Rico passed the ball to Saleem who ran with the ball. A player from the opponent's team tackled and kicked his leg, making him fall flat on the ground, wincing in pain.

The medical assistance team rushed to assist, but the damage was worse than everyone expected—he had broken his shinbone and needed to undergo emergency surgery as soon as possible.

That evening, Saleem hobbled back home on crutches. This ordeal scared his parents, but they wanted the best for him. So they took him to a specialist the next day to determine the next steps.

"You won't be able to play soccer again!" The specialist declared after the tests came back.

Saleem broke down and didn't understand why anyone would try to ruin his soccer career which had barely started.

The next few months were filled with sorrow, fear, regrets, and anxiety, but Saleem didn't quit. After undergoing surgery, he started going for therapy, hoping to recover promptly. He also practiced how to persevere without fear.

More months passed and he started getting worried. Despite being told he'd never play soccer again, he was still fiercely determined to recover and go back to the field, but his slow recovery process was making him lose hope.

On a fateful day, he went to the beach where he saw the old man who approached her, "Young Saleem, you can achieve whatever you put your focus on—nothing is impossible," He assured him. "Remember to persevere without fear."

These words stuck on Saleem's mind like super glue during the next few months, making him freeze any fears and try harder during all therapy sessions.

On a special day, he started walking on his broken leg and after a few days, he stopped using crutches.

Months passed and he was back to the field to practice. His determination shocked the teammates who thought they'd never see him play again.

Soon after, the truth came out—Rico had struck a deal with the opponent player to break Saleem's leg. Rico was removed from the team by the coach who started developing a deep sense of respect for Saleem as the most perseverant player, leader, and role model.

Eventually, due to his persistent efforts, he was made the team captain and his teammates also loved him deeply because he led them to victory so many times.

Years went by, and finally, he achieved his soccer dreams! He eventually won a scholarship to study while playing college soccer for an important team in Seattle.

Her parents were so proud and supported him throughout the process.

Saleem packed his bags, went to the shore to bid the old man goodbye, and impatiently waited for the next day.

He was too excited and could barely get any sleep that night. Finally, he was able to play for his dream team and from there, he'd grow to become the best player in the world.

The following day was gloomy; it felt as though the sky was also sad that he was moving to the other side of the country. All his teachers and teammates came to bid him tearful goodbyes at the airport.

It was Saleem's first time getting on the plane. He chose to sit by the window next to his mother.

"Mom, are you comfortable?" He asked politely.

"Yes, dear, and I'm so proud of you. You were able to achieve your dreams at a young age. I can't wait to see the amazing things you'll do next." She praised.

"Thanks, Mom," he replied.

"You're welcome, my love. With a little faith and confidence in yourself, you can go even further! Always strive to persevere without fear," is mother replied as the two embraced.

As the plane began taking off, Saleem felt excitement rushing through his athletic body. His mother gripped his arm to make sure he didn't feel too scared.

He was amazed by the views as the plane was up in the air. The world seemed so huge that the people below looked like ants; he couldn't wrap her head around the fact that each person had his or her own life.

After a few hours, the plane finally landed in lovely Seattle, Washington. As they arrived at their new house, he couldn't help but notice almost everyone in the new town was different.

The new town wasn't a colorful explosion like in diverse Detroit, but Saleem persevered and adapted quickly—he wouldn't let anything get in the way of his rainbow dreams of soccer and school success.

Learned lessons

Thank you, dear readers, for kicking it with smart and savvy Saleem today and uncovering the special life lesson that no matter who you are, what challenges you face, or what special needs you possess, there's nothing you cannot achieve in life, school, friendship, faith, or sports. We trust that you had a ball. Are you ready now to apply these motivational and mindful lessons each day as you strive for your own goals in life?

Despite the various physical, emotional, social, and spiritual hardships Saleem faced due to his poor vision, always recall how he bravely persevered without fear until he ultimately achieved his dreams and even served as a role model and a leader for his peers. Similarly, you should never give up on your own unique dreams, goals, aspirations, and objectives in life, no matter what!

After reading "Saleem's Mindful Miracle: Persevere Without Fear," let's take the time to try some final reflections and free bonus gift activities on your own to practice the character and life lessons mindfully from the sporty story. Feel free to ask an adult to assist you and have lots of fun together!

1. Saleem's Dream: Recall Saleem's special sports dream from the story. Then discuss what obstacles, special needs, or challenges he particularly faced when trying to achieve them. Do you encounter any obstacles, special needs, or challenges when attempting to obtain your own life goals, dreams, and aspirations? Briefly discuss. Create an action plan to overcome them as Saleem modelled

    _____

    _____

2. Persevere Without Fear Goal: Complete this sentence: I'll gladly persevere without fear today in order to improve at my sport by

    _____

    _____

3. Fast Forward: Draw, color, paint, or sketch a picture, collage, or visual of what it looks and feels like to persevere without fear in your life and future

    _____

    _____

4. Holler For Healing: What type of injury did Saleem sustain? How did he heal and recover? Did you ever

experience a sickness, injury, or physical setback? What happened? How did you personally persevere?

_____

_____

5. Persevere Cheer: Make a poem, rap, song, or cheer to remember what this important lesson implies.

_____

_____

CHAPTER 9

"Jharrel: Discover Perseverance, Healing, and Concentration"

As this endearing story creatively illustrates an inspiring tale about the journey of a tall, skilled, and driven young boy who aspires to become a top basketball player in Philadelphia, PA, USA, you'll most surely encounter lots of heartfelt ideas, educational crossovers, family matters, lifelong themes, and important steps to also emulate. Hit the courts and grab your shorts with this fun and empathetic adventure!

What's more, we'll further discuss empowering ways to explore sports themes, academic rigor, related vocabulary, and life lessons. You'll soon acquire how to overcome laziness, enjoy warmups and practice, apply procrastination, fizzle fears, love to exercise, and overcome challenging obstacles like loss and a family member's mental health challenges, just as Jharrel masters how to stop avoid practicing his craft.

Are you eager to join jumping Jharrel who will also lead you on a thrilling endeavor to change his family's overall lives? His story is so commendable and way more important than any basketball score, stat, or medal. This tale furthers offers relevant character education traits and brilliant life lessons related to hard work, perseverance, concentration, resilience, academic studies, school/sports balance, team work, courage, healing, and other attributes that propel us to success both on and off the courts!

If you are ready to examine a relatable story that will teach you how to focus fully on your own gifts, talents, hobbies, and strengths, how to plan ahead, show growth, learn from mistakes, succeed more at school, gain perseverance, and increase your focus and concentrate, then take a shot at this story with us now! Let's rapidly rebound together with school/sports/family balance and other socioemotional tips.

In brief, do you know what it means to dig down deep and find that special spark that we need to overcome our challenges and triumph on top? Well, it's called perseverance. This story will easily teach you to cheer and proactively persevere. Then you can swiftly improve and grow when you practice, concentrate, and challenge yourself. It also emphasizes why and how it's vital to maintain school/academic/sports/family balance and success in each area as well as how to cope with grief and loss and mental health challenges.

Moreover, as we dribble and shoot the ball with Jharrel, a gifted basketball prodigy, let's proactively observe how he applied focus, perseverance, grit, and a growth mindset, despite the fact that his path was initially filled with many obstacles. He models that when we keep our hearts and minds on the prize, we can fulfill our dreams, goals, objectives, and aspirations, regardless of how big, challenging, or impossible they may seem in this superb tale, "Jharrel: Discover Perseverance, Healing, and Concentration."

Based on this sweet story's abundance of lessons, you'll also uncover how Uncle Joe teaches the value of family and the significance of having a mentor or a coach on our side to motivate us. Whether you're medium, tall, or small, you can all have a ball after reading this enlightening tale.

Are you into clean, mindful, and healthy eating? This book also provides some beneficial points about health, exercise, wellness, and overall nutrition for young readers because Jharrel's mom was very focused on eating well.

Jharrel was the tallest boy in class since elementary school in Philadelphia, PA, USA.

Ever since he could crawl, he knew he wanted to be a professional basketball player. So, every day when he got home from school, he wore his jersey and shorts and went to the neighborhood court to practice with older kids. The best part was that he always impressively ended up scoring more points than they did.

Although Jharrel was still young, it was clear that he would one day change his parents' lives. Follow along as we score points in the powerful quest to acquire perseverance, a key to life and sports successes!

As mentioned, from a young age, Jharrel was top of his class. But as he grew, it became clear that Jharrel was not like other children. While they were short, he was overly tall; despite their love of playing outside, he preferred shooting hoops in the courtyard. Even though other kids wanted their parents to buy them different toys every week, Jharrel already had his favorite toy, which was his beloved basketball.

So every morning he would arrive at class earlier than other kids and head straight to the gym to practice by shooting hoops. Jharrel's parents tried their best to prepare him—it was clear that he was a child athletic prodigy. His talent in basketball was simply unmatched, even from such a tender age.

Because it was common for a prodigy to be given a personal coach, a lifelong mentor and friend, his family could not afford a fancy coach, they opted for Uncle Joe, who almost played professionally, but his injury halted his dreams.

"Jharrel! You need to put your head in the game!" Uncle Joe coached. Because despite being talented, the boy's mind would wander off often. Each evening, the duo went to the courtyard to practice without fail.

"Warm-ups are good for your body!" Uncle Joe emphasized.

"But they make my legs feel weak," Jharrel complained, hoping his excuses would save him, but Uncle Joe was a tough nut to crack.

Instead of going easy on him, Uncle Joe knew that the players who did not quit under pressure were the ones on their journey to becoming the best. In essence, he treasured the value of perseverance, healing, and concentration to win in life and basketball.

"Instead of four laps, you'll have to run five laps," Uncle Joe assigned and the boy would shrug, immediately hoping to change his uncle's mind. However, Uncle Joe's concentration was as strong as the sun's rays. After warm-ups, Uncle Joe would teach Jharrel new tricks to score points against his opponents.

Jharrel's dream was to be like Lebron James, so he practiced most of his signature moves and strategies. He also followed up on all his games and would study the icon's unique techniques.

While others were merely watching basketball, enjoying the game between two opponents, he would always have a notebook in hand, writing down everything worthwhile that he spotted, and went diligently to the court to practice the next day.

At home, Jharrel's mother prepared the best meals to ensure her son grew stronger with each passing day. She did this because she believed that strength came from the food we eat and everyone could choose to nourish their bodies.

In retrospect, Jharrel wanted to become a basketball player who played in the professional basketball league or NBA; and this made him push himself harder than ever, but often neglecting his studies.

"Jharrel, you'll need to put in more effort at school if you want us to keep supporting your dream." His father explained.

In turn, Jharrel promised to work harder in school because he understood that education was valuable. However, on that day, someone published his report card results and attached them to the community board. The other kids laughed at him.

"He'll never be a famous basketball player if he keeps failing at school," they jeered.

Turning away, he tried to ignore their laughter.

When Jharrel was 14, his father got ill and had to be rushed to the local health center. Shortly after, he was pronounced dead. This occurrence came as a shock to Jharrel who eventually had to take care of his mother because she quickly fell into a depressive state.

At this point, he had too many responsibilities on his plate. He had to balance his grades with basketball training while also taking care of himself since his mother was mentally unable.

These events made Jharrel weary. Ever since his dad passed away, things changed for the worse. He did not know how to help his mother who was getting sadder by the day and eventually had to be checked into a mental institution after being diagnosed with Clinical Depression.

He longed to honor his father's wishes, so he studied hard while still playing basketball. At first, he was selected for the junior team but due to his extraordinary abilities, he was shortly selected to play in the main team despite being the youngest player.

Still, Uncle Joe, who was now catering to Jharrel as his legal guardian, kept pushing him to be the best version of himself with each passing day.

"Practice makes perfect," Uncle Joe repeated. "You need to turn that hurt into something beautiful. There's more than one path to greatness," he reminded. "Prioritize your studies as well, Jharrel," he patiently advised.

One day, Jharrel went to visit and saw his mother crying.

"Why are you crying, Mother?" he asked.

"I'm worried about you, Jharrel," she answered. "Soon, you'll grow to be a man, and I'm still not yet to be released because of this sadness that gripped me."

Jharrel did try to cheer her up by taking her to the courtyard at the institution and showing her his new tricks.

"You'll be the best basketball player in the world!" She cheered as she tearfully watched him.

"Are you eating well?" She asked. "Is Uncle Joe offering nourishing food instead of that junk stuff like Twinkies and Oreos?" She giggled.

"Yes, Uncle Joe is the best!" Jharrel replied as he smiled.

Their encounter was cut short because he had to practice. Yet seeing his mother uplifted Jharrel's spirit more than ever before and this time he promised to strive harder and persevere for greatness.

Two years passed by and at Jharrel's request, Uncle Joe decided to let him join a special basketball program where Jharrel would be coached by the elite instructors. Jharrel began to take small steps even though he'd been practicing since he was small. With time, his physique changed; his hands and legs grew stronger and he could do things the boys at school could not achieve. It was a long road, but Jharrel was surprised and pleased by his steady progress.

As time passed, Jharrel eventually mastered his technique which was crucial for any professional player. He grew stronger than the pain he felt! His confidence outshined any fears or doubts that had formerly stifled him.

Everyone at school was shocked; he scored so many points during basketball games, leading the team to victory time and time again. His family was also amazed, especially his mother.

The people wondered, "How's he doing all this? How's he playing like a star at such a young age?" They all felt like he would soon be like Lebron James. Jharrel's talent even seemed to outshine all his peers and this success made some players angry.

Perhaps, he could be the best after all?

At school, some of his teammates were jealous over Jharrel's achievements. They felt overshadowed by his growing success—especially the older kids. How could a young boy lead them to victory all the time? Was there a possibility he would get the scholarship to college instead of them? Furthermore, their worries worsened since he was gaining recognition throughout Philadelphia for his community and academic efforts, not just on the courts.

This angered the seniors. Because they wanted their place back, they began treating Jharrel poorly, making life difficult for him, but the young boy persevered with confidence, concentration, and healing. This reaction did not make them happy either—they wanted to crush the boy's spirit, so he would quit the basketball team.

Seeing how Jharrel kept prospering despite his adversities, the seniors crafted an evil plan to hurt Jharrel, but the coach caught onto it, expelling the boys before they did anything.

"You don't have to worry, Jharrel. When others see greatness, they often selfishly want it for themselves and that's why they try to hurt others because they cannot get what they want. Hurt people hurt people," the coach calmly explained.

The coach observed the boys during a team meeting and noticed the animosity and resentment some teammates carried. They were afraid of Jharrel's potential.

Soon after, he kept an eye on the boys and eventually found them making plans to hurt Jharrel again, so he had to take action and remove the boys from the team.

As a result, the boys were not happy with this. Besides, they were seniors as well, and being kicked off the team was not good for their SATs. It only made their admission to college more complicated.

Jharrel was thankful to the coach, but he felt guilty for what the seniors were going through. Regardless, he couldn't help them since he had his own goals to achieve and had to focus on his own life and his mother's needs.

After a while, his mother's health declined and he had to start working to provide money for her treatment. Balancing basketball, school work, family and a job were hectic tasks—he started missing basketball practice and soon he was kicked out of the special program and school team.

This demotivated him so much since he had given everything to becoming a professional basketball player. His mother passed away during his final exams and his whole world came crashing down. Uncle Joe tried his best to help, him but he could only do so much! He lacked a stable job to support him, so Jharrel decided to move out.

The results came out and he scored at the top of his class. Shortly after, he attended a prestigious university where he tried to join the basketball team but was rejected during the first tryouts since he was not in top shape and had not played basketball competitively in a while.

Next, he remembered how he used to be the best since elementary school and he dedicated his time to studying and basketball. He used to spend so many hours in the courtyard; so much so that the coach had to tell him to go home and rest.

During the next audition, he tried his luck once again and he was added to the team. From then, he decided that the only way was up. He gave basketball his all and was eventually scouted to play for a regional team, where he contributed a lot of wins. His potential impressed numerous teams and was offered an opportunity to play for a national league, which he agreed to as long as they allowed him to still finish his degree.

Accordingly, he began to live the life of his dreams but deep down he felt sad because his parents were not there to celebrate his success with him. Instead, he celebrated his success with others who needed his help like Uncle Joe and the kids who were facing adversities at a young age as he did.

Jharrel soon became a beacon of strength and success in his community due to never giving up, concentrating, healing, persevering, and pushing forward, regardless of the setbacks he experienced in his life.

Learned lessons

Just as Jharrel realized that the only way in life was up after encountering so much strife and stress, it's so vital that you, too, can shoot for your life's goals, dreams, objectives, and aspirations as well. Like a ladder to the stars, you can climb slowly and steadily toward success with concentration, perseverance, and healing.

Do you ever face challenges like Jharrel did? How did you cope and overcome them? In fact, your problems should only make you stronger, just like Jharrel, as he proactively dealt with stress, adversity, and obstacles like school and family problems, grief and loss, money problems, lack of concentration, and so on.

Yet as the story clearly illustrated, we must never give up on our dreams and show up every day to work on them, despite any roadblocks or negative situations at home, school, or community. Where you're from doesn't ever fully define you, as Jharrel successfully showed. If you can dream it, you can surely achieve it, as he did in so many facets of his young life and career!

Don't forget the abundant lessons from "Jharrel: Discover Perseverance, Healing, and Concentration." It echoes how hard work, perseverance, concentration, resilience, courage, healing, and other character education traits can lead us to success both on and off the courts!

If you're ready to apply some of the story's tips, then complete these fun, free exercises and extensions now:

1. Picture of Perseverance. This story showed how to gain and sustain perseverance. Therefore, draw or sketch a picture of a time when you applied perseverance at home, school, sports, or community involvement. What did it look and feel like to you?

   _____

   _____

2. Living With Loss: Jharrel sadly lost both parents at young ages. Did you ever lose a pet, a toy, or a family member? How do you keep the memory of your beloved alive? Discuss 2-3 ways.

   _____

   _____

3. City of Brotherly Love: Identify the story's setting in terms of city, state, and country.

_____

_____

4. Basketball Legends: Research 2-3 of the sport's famous stars from around the world by going online with an adult's permission or help or checking out a book about this topic from your school or your local library.

_____

_____

5. Food Fun: Jharrel's mom advocated proper nutrition and healthy eating. What's your 2-3 favorite HEALTHY foods to consume? Why?

_____

_____

CHAPTER 10

"Caden's Crown of Confidence and Champion Mindset: Don't Mess With the King of Chess!"

Do you want to get your game on today as far as chess games that promote strategy, patience, and wit? Then you'll enjoy meeting a new friend named Caden, a young, bright, and curious boy from a small town in Utah, USA, yearns to earn the coveted title as the best chess player in the world, despite a historical ban on chess. He feels so different and alone from all others because no one can relate to his unique aspirations and passions in life. He starts to question if his dream is really a pawn or is it possible?

In retrospect, this harsh legal restriction dated back to the 1800s in Europe due to religious reasons and was brought to America by the immigrants. Yet despite this unfortunate occurrence and close-minded policy, he doesn't give up and sets on a journey to find a safe, accepting, and creative place where he can play freely. This royal quest takes clever Caden to places he never thought he'd go. Cheer him on and learn along with him as he moves from stalemate to great.

Are you ready to explore valuable life lessons and essential character traits such as discipline, a champion mindset, and confidence that will also make you feel as majestic as a monarch? Do you desperately need the critical skills and practical strategies to shine with individuality and not give in to peer pressure? "Caden's Crown of Confidence and Champion Mindset: Don't Mess With the King of Chess!" delivers an inspirational tale of wit, patience, individuality, discipline, courage, strength, and confidence.

Have you ever felt like a black sheep, vastly different from others in your classroom, family, or sports team because your goals or expectations weren't the same as theirs? Well, practice your royal courtesy right now because this helpful story will equip you with so many life lessons and vital character traits to swiftly, freely, mindfully, and successfully win at the game of life, chess, family dynamics, culture, religion, or whatever sport, hobby, goal, or dream you're desiring.

"Caden's Crown of Confidence and Champion Mindset: Don't Mess With the King of Chess!" delivers an inspirational tale of wit, patience, individuality, courage, strength, and confidence.

Will Caden break the shackles of the past and discover the discipline and creativity to march toward his desires?

In the first place, what is confidence? Like wearing a cape or a jewelled crown, confidence refers to the feeling or belief that one can rely on someone, oneself, or something. It's that deep inner trust and fire of faith that it can happen.

Along the same lines, this inspirational story also presents what it means to embrace a champion mindset. What does this entail exactly? As you know, champions are like warrior as they confidently think, speak, and act like winners. So if you can believe it, you can achieve it. Let's explore this fascinating tale and determine how Caden applies confidence and a champion mindset to fulfil his goals. You can then start applying these life lessons to your own favorite sport, hobby, passion, or goals.

It began as a warm and wonderful July day in a tiny town near Salt Lake City, Utah, USA. Everyone was content with their lives—well, everyone except a curious, charming, and clever country boy named Caden. While most other kids in the rural town aspired to be farmers or laborers, he dreamt of playing chess professionally. Every so often, Caden would tinker away into the attic and play alone for hours upon hours, daydreaming about being the world's best at chess.

The problem that Caden faced in pursuing his chess dream was a lofty and a historical one. King Louis the 9th had banned chess, calling it a boring game. So if anyone was caught playing, they would be charged a hefty fine or sentenced to life in the dungeon. While Caden was a boy of modern times, his town was sadly stuck in the Dark Ages still when it came to new laws and open-minded policies. Instead of promoting individuality, Caden's town tugged toward conformity in the tug-of-war of creative freedoms of expressions and choices.

The town's many chess fans who eventually dropped the sport as a result of the ban. No one was brave enough to risk it—well, except for courageous Caden. He was super passionate about chess and was the secret chess champion at his school, which was a school of one since he was home-schooled. There was nothing more he yearned for than becoming a world chess champion and with his advanced but undercover skills, this goal wasn't impossible.

One day, Caden gathered up the courage and confessed to his mother about his desired dream. "Mom, Why can't I play chess outside this house? Why doesn't the State like the game?" Caden asked politely.

His mild-mannered mother was quite shocked by Caden's bold question. She thought her son had gracefully accepted the sealed fate based on the ban. "Be careful, Cade! The walls have ears!" She whispered.

"Why did the King make such a decision and why are we still following it in these modern times?" Caden asked.

"Because he hates chess and all change, for that matter. Religion and chess have never coexisted properly." Mother replied.

"But—I want to play chess and hopefully one day I'll attend the World Championship in Japan!" Caden enthusiastically expressed.

"Oh, my darling! There's nothing I want more than for you to experience the world how you want it, but sometimes the reality is harsher than we expect," Caden's mother warned.

"I'll look for a way to leave this boring town and follow my dream!" He proclaimed proudly.

The next day as soon as he finished eating his big bowl of Cheerios, Caden made his way to his former mentor's house to ask how he could attend the National Championship.

"Since the ban on chess is still imposed, there can't be any national games," Joe announced. "The World Chess Federation (WCF) won't register a small town player, so I'm very sorry, Caden." Joe continued.

As result, Caden sat still and sulked in steely silence. All he wanted was to play chess and use this opportunity to change the world positively. However, that goal was hard to achieve because of the ban's close-minded thinking and focus on conformity.

For a fleeting moment, Caden's cotton candy dreams of playing chess seemed too hard to achieve. He just couldn't believe he had to change the course of his life just because a piece of paper deemed chess as rebellious or boring.

"Remember, no matter how hard some things may seem, sometimes there's truly the light at the end of the tunnel, " Joe reminded.

"But what can I do, Joe?" Caden asked eagerly.

"You'll find a way, one step at a time" Joe calmly replied.

"Can you tell me what to do? I cannot give up now!" Caden insisted.

"At your young age, you shouldn't be tied up to one passion, so you still have time to develop more interests, gain confidence, and express your individuality," Joe asserted.

"It's as though you're hiding something. Why aren't you being clear with me? Why are you beating about the bush?" Caden asked.

"Little one, you're still young. You shouldn't let anyone dictate your choices," Joe encouraged.

"Like a game of chess itself, I feel like you aren't being clear with me. You keep going back and forth. Should I fight for my dreams or not?" Caden asked curiously.

"That's for your heart to decide. You can achieve anything you set your mind upon. It's called a champion mindset. If you think, speak, and act like a winner, you'll truly be one. All it takes is the discipline and confidence to unlock this treasure chest of tools," Joe declared.

The sunset danced across the sky and confused Caden went back home. He barely touched his mashed potatoes at dinner and went straight to bed. Despite trying to sleep, he couldn't snooze a bit that night.

Instead, all he could think about was how he could play chess, so he dashed to the attic and secretively played solo all night long.

The following day the sun rose, flickering bright rays of light through the attic's window, reminding him that morning had arrived. Caden tiptoed back to his room and locked himself in—it was hard to believe he was still living a nameless chess champion. He felt like he'd been reduced to nothing since it prohibited to share beyond his attic walls.

Caden ate his breakfast and went to the den for home-school where he was reminded that he couldn't play chess anymore. His days began feeling the same and he felt as though there was no way out of the boredom he was experiencing. He lacked discipline and felt super restless.

How ironic! Chess was banned because the ruling class felt it was boring, but now Caden was bored because he couldn't play chess anymore.

So the day ended pretty quickly, and he went to the mountains to relax. The outdoors had a special way to ease his agony.

As soon as he sat on a rock, he heard footsteps behind.

"Young Caden?" The strange voice asked.

"Yes." He replied. "How can I help you?" He added.

"Most of the chess enthusiasts left the American West, so they moved to the East to seek freedom," The man replied.

"Where's this place?" Caden asked.

"It's a safe haven for people who want to play chess, express discipline, shine confidence, and adopt a champion mindset. They won't be stopped by the mere whims of any old school law," the man revealed.

"How can I get there?" Caden asked.

"You can wait until 11 pm. There's a train that leaves each night at the station," the man informed.

"Thank you!" Caden replies. His excitement took the best of him. This was truly the glimpse of hope he was yearning for! No matter what, he had to save money so he could move to this safe haven for chess players.

In the meantime, he chose to work at the local market to save money for his big move. Since he heard the news of a way to follow his passion, the spark in his eyes came back and it shone brighter than ever, making him a strong, confident believer in the champion mindset.

Seasons passed by, and finally, she had the money she needed to leave town.

Then on a chilly afternoon, he sat by the window pane, waiting for his mom to arrive so he could explain everything to her and ask for her blessing before he went to chase his cheerful chess dream.

"Mom, I found a way," he confessed.

"What do you mean, my son?" Caden's mother replied.

"I found a way to play chess again," he confirmed.

"That again! I can't afford to pay the fine. Don't break the rules!" His mother warned.

"But—" Caden tried to explain, but his mother intervened.

"I know you adore the sport, but we cannot break the rules!" Caden's mother cautioned.

"I have to," he insisted.

"I don't think I can handle losing you." His mother admitted.

You won't lose me, Mama, but I have to confidently follow my heart and hope that using discipline and a champion mindset, my actions will change other people's lives who are afraid," he exclaimed.

At this point, Caden realized he had to leave town and follow his dreams, despite the disapproval from his mother. He hoped that one day, she would understand.

Once his mother fell into a deep slumber, Caden packed his bags and patiently waited to leave the following day. He was too excited and couldn't sleep, so he went to the attic to play chess. Suddenly, she heard footprints approaching and hid his board and pieces.

"I'm here to play," Caden's mother whispered.

"Mom? You know how to play?" Caden's asked in excitement.

"Where do you think you learned the sport? You used to watch me all the time when you were a baby," his mother replied.

The two played and Caden's mother won.

"You have to teach me!" Caden begged.

"Of course! I've also decided to go with you. I'll support you through every step of the way," his smart mother assured.

Accordingly, Caden felt a deep sense of peace, confidence, and discipline. Finally, he had the only support he truly needed.

The following day was gloomy, but it ended pretty quickly. The duo had prepared for their journey and arrived on time at the station, allowing the carriage to take them. After a few hours, they finally arrived in the East.

As Caden entered this new world of freedom and creativity, she breathed a sigh of relief. It was the start—but an important beginning. The town wasn't like their town—there was more individuality and people did what they wanted.

"So, what brought you here?" A delicate voice asked.

Caden turned around and saw a man holding a shiny chess board.

He immediately pulled him to the side and started whispering, "You should hide that before anyone sees you!"

The man let out a loud laugh.

"Why are you laughing?" Caden asked curiously.

"This region is free, so I can carry the board," he added.

The man accompanied Caden and his mother to a huge house that had numerous rooms. They were given a comfortable room and got a chance to meet other chess players.

After resting, Caden was summoned to the playroom where he met the head of the center.

"So, what brings you here?" She asked.

"I love chess and I want to be in the World Championship in Japan," Caden replied.

"Alright! We'll see!" The woman stated and walked away.

To pass the time, Caden and his mother practiced chess all the time. He even began signing up for competitions and won them all effortlessly, making the whole town know him.

On a fateful day, he signed up for an important competition and once he auditioned, he secured a spot.

It turned out that the competition was the National League and the World Chess Federation (WFC) was actually hosting it. Caden was given the spot on one condition, so no one would ever know where he originated from as far as his native citizenship.

The competition would to be held across the Atlantic Ocean in England; and Caden's journey would begin in the morning. His mother would also accompany him.

That night, he couldn't sleep. It was hard to believe that his goals were falling into place simply because he took a major step he'd been scared of initially. He praised his ability to acquire and show confidence as well as his champion mindset for his success thus far.

His mother could sense his anxiety, so she came to keep him company and soon after, they both fell asleep.

The sun rose the following day. Caden woke up and prepared for the European journey. His peers wished him luck before they journeyed to England.

As they arrived, he marveled at the sight of the British flag that could be seen almost everywhere. The streets were filled with passers-by who were busy and didn't have time for 'hellos' or 'goodbyes.'

They soon checked in at the lavish hotel. Caden had never seen anything like it—the room was huge; bigger than their house in Utah. The moment he was having was a result of choosing to be brave, confident, and optimistic. Mother congratulated Caden for reaching new heights in socioemotional skills.

The day in London was lovely. They enjoyed breakfast while looking at the view of London Bridge. Caden photographed the memory deep inside his brain.

The next day was the Nationals and he was totally prepared. His opponent was overly prideful because he had never lost a match and he believed it was easier for him since Caden was new to the tournament. But the match wasn't easy; and just when he was about to move the wrong piece, he changed her mind and that small shift in action led to Caden's victory.

In essence, he was celebrated around Europe and the next stop would soon be Japan to play the finals. Caden's chess name had become like a famous song. It was chartered by many who believed he would bring the trophy for the first time to America.

The days flashed by so fast, that he had a team of expert players who practiced with Caden day and night. Japan was known to produce the best chess players but this time, Europe and America hoped to take the crown.

Days passed by and it was time to go to Japan for the finals. Once they arrived, Caden supressed tears of joy. After acquiring confidence and a champion mindset, he proudly took the chance and was living his biggest dreams.

Like England's hub of activities, Tokyo, Japan also had so much hustle and bustle. The people spoke a different language and it was seemingly harder than the language British people spoke. But despite all the adversities as a visitor, Caden wanted to make his nation and his mother proud.

The day of the finals commenced and all the players were assembled in a playroom. Players across the continents began to fail one after the other until two were left; Asia and North America. So Caden sat with his opponent and studied every move he made. He also carefully analyzed every step. While most people deemed the Japanese as the best chess players; they were right.

This was the toughest game Caden had ever played. Whenever he thought he made the winning move or a move that would bring him closer to triumph, his opponent proved Caden wrong.

What was worse, the opponent did it so calmly-as if it was so easy for him. His attitude eventually became his downfall because Caden analyzed him carefully and caught up to him. Then just as when he thought Caden would make a move that would bring him victory, he did the opposite of what was expected and ended up victorious.

All in all, Caden was the first American boy to win the championship against the best players from each continent. His victory was followed by celebrations all over Europe. Even the King of France was intrigued. The tension of the game caught the attention of all the nations, marking it as an important occasion.

Eventually, Caden was awarded the trophy. When he was asked about the nation he represented, he confidently answered that he was from a small town near Utah, USA.

How could a boy from a country that banned chess be the world chess champion?

Learned lessons

Regardless of how impossible a situation might seem to you at first, it's so important for you to remember this stunning story and its major takeaway points. It reminds us that there's always a way out and a possible path to pursue your greatest dreams. As the story illustrated, you just have to find it.

Similarly, the life lesson in this tale also reiterates how we must never settle and always choose your own destiny. Like a recipe, you just need some basic ingredients as this tale discussed: confidence, focus, creativity, and a champion mindset. As Caden and his mother demonstrated so clearly to us, you never know where an ounce of bravery can take you—Japan, maybe? Arigato!

Pause now and get your post-reading game on as you complete interactive reflections and free bonus gift exercises to apply the character and life lessons from the story to your own life.

1. Word Wise: Define "restriction" using context clues from the story. Explain why chess was restricted for Caden. Try creating an original sentence using this word.

_____

_____

2. Character Class: Reflect on the three key terms of discipline, a champion mindset, and confidence featured in this story. Name someone in your life who models each trait. Explain why and how he or she models this virtue so well

_____

_____

3. Title Times: Although the author chose "Caden's Crown of Confidence and Champion Mindset: Don't Mess With the King of Chess!" as the story's title. Now imagine you're making a movie version of this story. What title will you choose to name it? Why? Which famous actors/actresses would you cast for the lead characters?

_____

_____

4. Confidence Corner: With your parents' permission, create a confidence corner in one area of your home where

you can go to relax, take a deep breath, meditate, pray, read, draw, or engage in any other activity that builds your confidence.

_____

_____

5. Chess History: Although this book is fiction, expand your research and history skills now by researching online or check out a book from your local library about when and where chess began.

_____

_____

CONCLUSION

Based on reading these superb stories, you're now fully equipped to address all the numerous, complex, challenging, and stressful problems, themes, situations, and obstacles in life. The ball is in your court now to apply these character education and life lesson as you navigate through life and transition from a boy to a man.

Just as athletes use helmets, pads, uniforms, and equipment to safeguard their minds, bodies, and souls during athletic feats, this book serves as your guide to act, speak, and think more mindfully, morally, intentionally, happily, healthily, and ethically.

We've given you relatable and authentic characters to serve as mirrors and reflect all the vital topics and life lessons, so you can win at any goal that you pursue!

Plus, after completing all the post-reading activities and exercises, you'll triumph with persistence, focus, self-belief, bravery, concentration, healing, determination, grit, resilience, a growth and champion mindset, confidence, and other necessary social skills in your toolbox.

You'll be able to exhibit more leadership qualities and be able to master how and why practice is a powerhouse trait in sports and life. By showcasing your newfound attitude of gratitude, optimism, collaboration, empathy, friendship and family loyalty, you'll soon score and soar at whatever objectives or dreams that you desire in swimming, chess, boxing, figure skating, soccer, cycling, surfing, hockey, and all sporty areas of life!

Thank You

Thank you very much for picking up a copy of my book.

You could have chosen from a variety of different books, but you decided to take a chance and go with this one. so, thank you for purchasing this book and reading on it to the conclusion.

Before you leave, I'd like to request a tiny favor from you. Could you please consider leaving an Amazon review? The greatest and simplest way to promote independent authors like me is to write a review. Your input will assist me in continuing to write the types of books that will assist you in achieving the results you desire. It would mean a lot to me if you could let me know your opinion.

Made in the USA
Columbia, SC
09 October 2023

24201559R00085